His Living Sculpture

Inspired by the Holy Spirit
WRITTEN BY ANDREA MINGS

Copyright © 2013 by Andrea Mings

His Living Sculpture
by Andrea Mings

Printed in the United States of America

ISBN 9781626979772

All rights reserved solely by the author. The author guarantees all contents are original and do not infringe upon the legal rights of any other person or work. No part of this book may be reproduced in any form without the permission of the author. The views expressed in this book are not necessarily those of the publisher.

Unless otherwise indicated, Bible quotations are taken from the King James version of the Bible. Copyright © 1976 by Thomas Nelson, Inc.

www.xulonpress.com

TABLE OF CONTENTS

Introduction	v
A Memoir: From Father to Father	9
The Devine Connection:	
Crossing the Bridge	25
The Bridge	29
The Gray Figures ~ The Battles	34
Light Expels the Darkness	40
The Connection	42
My Calling:	
A Nun In The Protestant Church	47
When I Said No To God	56
Finally, I Said Yes To God	62
Rejection Survivor	65
The Journey to Discover My Assignment	83
In Loving Memory of My Parents	92
The Other Side of Death	95

INTRODUCTION

*G*iving glory and honor to God, I thank Father God for bringing me here in this life and for loving me and giving me new life: I am a born-again believer in Jesus Christ. I am a child of God. I am a friend of Jesus and He is my Husband. I am chosen of God and dearly loved. I am a partaker of His heavenly calling. And it is only by the grace of God I am who I am. I also thank my parents for doing the best they could with what little they had in this life. Most of all, I thank You ♥Holy Spirit♥ for the work You have been doing in me. In my younger years, I was abused and neglected. As a young child, one time my mother punished me for a whole year, she used to beat me unmercifully, or just cry because she could not handle life's pressures after my father passed away.

As a teenager, my mother withdrew into herself. She got up every morning, went to work, came home and stayed in her bedroom; therefore, I was abandoned. I had to take care of myself and survive in the wild. One day, after I was baptized in the Holy Spirit in June 1978, God said He was going to domesticate me. The Miriam Webster definition of the word "domesticate" is to bring into domestic use; to adapt (an animal or plant) to life in intimate association with and to the advantage of humans. The word "domestic" means to TAME, DOMESTICATE <the *domestic*

cat>. In other words, God was saying that I was wild and He was going to tame me. I titled this book *His Living Sculpture* because I felt as if ♥God the Holy Spirit♥ had to literally break me down and remake me, start all over again from the inside out. Many of us started with very rough beginnings. My story makes me think of an Old Testament time when the sons of Israel were in Egypt after Joseph died.

Scripture says in Exodus 1: 8, "Now, a new king arose over Egypt who did not know Joseph." Joseph had found favor with the old king, but the new king didn't know Joseph and feared that the Israelites were "too many". Consequently, this king decided to enslave the Israelites. Verse fourteen says, "This made their lives bitter." Because of this bitter life, the people cried out to God for help and God sent Moses with an escape plan. Through Moses, God delivered the Israelites out of Egypt, but it was very hard for them to change their way of thinking. Scripture also says, "My people perish for lack of knowledge." Even though I had accepted Jesus as my Savior at an early age, I was without knowledge; consequently, I lived a life of sin–the bitter life. I was miserable and angry, and as a result, through the years, I cried out for deliverance, an escape from the life I was living. Jesus rescued me out of the sinful life; however, the anger in me had already turned to bitterness; therefore, I hated life. Then the work of the ♥Holy Spirit♥ started.

Because of the bitterness, it was hard for me to change my way of thinking about life. I so desperately wanted to change my circumstances, not knowing that change had to start on the inside – my soul. Consequently, I developed a plan to change my life, but whenever I felt stressed, I used to yell, "I hate life! Then I would throw tantrums by tearing up paper or just finding things to throw away. Here is a story of a damsel who was in distress and her Hero, Jesus, by the Holy Spirit of God, came and rescued her. This is a story of my life in the Potter's hand, and He ain't through with me yet.

A Memoir: From Father to Father

*I*n December 1960, Andrew Leroy Mings, veteran of the United States Army and a security guard at Holmesburg State Prison in Pennsylvania, died of a brain tumor, leaving his wife, Lillian Josephine and two daughters, Rochelle Antoinette and Andrea Denise. My sister was seven years old at the time, and I was five years old. I did not understand much of what was going on, but something on the inside of me had left with him. On the day of the funeral, my family and I sat on the first pew in the church for the viewing at Lombard Central Presbyterian Church in West Philadelphia. I gazed at the shiny, dark brown coffin the whole time I was sitting there. After the pastor performed the service, my mother, my sister, and I were ushered over to the coffin to say goodbye. Somebody picked me up so that I could see my father. I saw him lying there with a lot of make-up on his face, dressed in a nice black suit. Also, inside the coffin was satiny white and there was white lace around the satin white pillow. The ushers caught my sister when she tried to crawl into my father's coffin.

After the viewing, we went to the cemetery somewhere in Washington, DC. Because it was a military funeral, there were soldiers in navy-blue uniforms and white gloves. They shot their weapons in the air, folded a flag, and gave it to my mother. After the funeral, we were escorted to my parent's house. I sat on the steps in my living room that led to the second floor of the house and watched my family, neighbors, and the funeral director as they hovered over my mother because she grieved so deeply that she fainted. Then the funeral director placed a small bottle of green crystals, called smelling salt, under her nose, which awakened her. After this sorrowful event, my mother continued with our family rituals, but it just wasn't the same without my father. She had to become mother and father to her children.

In 1954, a year before I was born, my parents bought a house in a well-kept, quiet neighborhood of red brick, two-story row houses on 57th and Samson Streets in West Philadelphia. They moved into the house when my sister was one year old. Samson Street was wide enough to park about three cars side by side. The friendly neighbors kept their property clean and their gardens full of flowers. They always greeted each other with a friendly "Hello" and a smile. On my side of Samson Street was a driveway that led to the back of the houses. If you walked on the driveway, you would pass by the back of the houses on one side of the driveway that had thirteen steps that led to the back door of the houses, which led to the kitchen. Under the steps was the door to the basement, and next to that was the one-car garage. There was a four-story garage for car repairs and an auto-body shop on the other side of the driveway. About ten feet from there was the back of Acme Supermarket. At the end of the driveway, there was a waist high wall where one could see the back of the houses on 58th Street. Children played on Samson Street or they rode their bikes on the driveway. The parents were proud of our neighborhood and as I recall, it was a peaceful place to live.

Also in 1954, my family–my maternal grandparents, a few cousins, and my parents with my sister – used to take one day trips to Atlantic City, NJ. In April, 1955, my parents brought home another little baby girl–me. My mother said that I was a very happy baby and easy to take care of. She also said I was my father's favorite, so here I am with my father's name–Andrea. When I was a toddler, I remember we stayed home on the weekends. One ritual my mother had was to get up early on Saturday mornings to open all the windows in the house and to open the front door in the living room and the back door in the kitchen. She enjoyed allowing the sunshine and the morning breeze to enter the house. After my sister and I were awakened, dressed, and fed by my mother, my father would watch over us while my mother attended to her family with her household chores and shopping.

One morning, after breakfast, when my mother went downstairs into the basement to wash clothes, my father sat my sister and me on the couch in the living room. Then he went into the kitchen and drank some water. While my sister and I watched him from the living room couch, he pretended to slowly transform into the famous fictional gigantic ape from the movie *King Kong*. Apparently, they must've watched the movie the night before because when he walked into the living room acting like the gigantic ape, my sister screamed and ran to get away from him. I was clueless as to what was going on, so I just followed my sister's lead and ran to the dining room to sit under the table. I guess that was my safety zone. My sister continued to run and scream around the dining room table until my mother yelled, "Stop the noise!" Since playtime was over, my father allowed my sister and me to go outside and play on the front porch. He used to play his classical and calypso albums on the High Fidelity, known as "Hi-Fi", stereo.

We had another family ritual on Sunday mornings. My family and I attended Sunday services at Lombard Central Presbyterian Church on the corner of 42nd Street and Powelton Avenue. Every Sunday, after arriving home, my mother would take my sister and me to our bedroom to change our clothes so we could eat lunch. Then we could sit in the living room to watch television or go outside to play on the porch. Unfortunately, there's not much more I can remember from my very early childhood about my father, except the fact that during the week, he used to come home from work with headaches. My mother said that I used to run and get his slippers from my parent's bedroom. I remember that the ache in his head was so painful that sometimes he couldn't hold his head up. It wasn't too long after the doctors discovered he had a brain tumor when he died in the hospital December 1960. In either February or March of 1961, my mother said that the pastor of the church flirted with her; therefore, she decided to stop going to church, but she sent her children to Richardson Memorial Presbyterian Church located at 59th and Walnut Streets, which was closer to the house. Therefore, the Sunday ritual ended.

My mother used to get us up on Sunday mornings, tell us to get dressed, and be on time for Sunday school. When we didn't move fast enough, she used to yell and push us to move faster and push us out of the house. One notable Passover Sunday, April 2, 1961, four months after my father passed away, I sat in my Sunday school class and listened intently while my teacher talked about Jesus. I thought He was a very nice man and I wanted to meet Him. After my teacher handed my classmates and me little scripture cards that had a picture representing Jesus on it, I gazed at the picture until everything faded in the background and my teacher's voice became muffled. Then, starting from my head, I felt as if I was being engulfed and slowly placed into a bubble. I was only six years old at the time, so I did not understand what had happened; therefore, I kept it to myself. After Sunday services, my sister and I used to walk home from church, change our clothes, make our lunch and eat, then my sister and I used to go outside to sit on the chairs on the front porch.

That afternoon, our next door neighbor's daughter and granddaughter came to visit my neighbor. Before the granddaughter, who was about my age at that time, entered the house, she looked at me and asked, "Are you saved?" Before I could give her my answer, a voice said to me, "Wait till you get older." So I said to her, "I don't know"; therefore, she decided not to stay outside and play. Again, I didn't understand what happened. About a year later, after that experience in my life, one day, my mother asked my sister and me if we wanted to continue to go to church. Well, of course, we said, "No". I was tired of being yelled at for being late for Sunday school and church. Therefore, on Sundays, completely forgetting what had happened to me on that Passover Sunday 1961, we stopped going to church. As far as family relations, we stopped visiting my paternal grandmother and family on Sundays and my aunt and cousins stopped visiting us.

In 1961, I started attending Hamilton Elementary School. In 1962, my mother started working; therefore, during the week, we went to the baby sitter's house after school. For a while my mother picked us up from the baby sitter's, brought us home, cooked dinner then retreated to her bedroom. After my sister and I ate our dinner, we had to put the food away and clean the kitchen. If our chores and homework were finished, then we could go outside and play with our friends. We either played outside together on each other's porches or we would visit each other's homes. We shared our toys and played games together peacefully. Starting in the summer of 1963, my mother continued taking one day trips to meet family in Atlantic City, NJ. She used to rise up early before daybreak to pack the car with clothes and food. Then she would wake my sister and me to get us washed and dressed. We thought she was crazy for waking us when it was still dark outside. Then she used to pack the trunk of her light blue 1956 Chevy Impala (nick-named Old Betsy), put my sister and me in the back seat, and leave for AC for the whole day.

In the mid-sixties, my mother stopped sending my sister and me to the babysitter's house, but we were told to go straight home from school. This changed our lives and affected our family relations. A spirit of violence and chaos entered our house. The fun loving mother had become stressed and angry. My friendship with my sister was ruined; she became hateful towards me. My mother would come home from work, put the dinner on the stove or in the oven, and then forget it. As a result, many dinners were burned. After dinner, my sister and I had to clean the kitchen. We took turns washing the dishes, scrubbing the pots, and sweeping the kitchen floor. That was tough for two girls in elementary school.

After we cleaned the kitchen, we had to do our homework, take our baths, and go to bed. Without us knowing it, while we were sleeping, my mother used to inspect the dishes. Whenever she found any dish that wasn't clean enough, she used get her belt, come in our bedroom, and hit us with the belt until we woke up. I remember one time asking, "What happened? What did I do?" She yelled back, "Go down stairs and rewash those dishes!" I can remember when there were nights I was up so late that it was hard to get up the next morning for school, and if I was late for school, I was beaten. This also affected my grades in school. I can remember a few report card seasons when I received a year of punishment or beaten for low grades. My mother used to put my head between her legs and hold my hands behind my back and beat me with a belt as she called it "unmercifully."

While my mother used the calf of her legs to hold my head, several times I tried to turn my head so that I could bite her, but she held my head so tight that I could not turn to defend myself and get away from her. So whenever she wanted to beat me, I used to run for my life. Then she would threaten me by saying if she caught me while running then the beating would be worse. There were other times when she used to tell us to walk over to her while she sat on the couch, to bend over, so she could slap us in the face. I heard my sister ask, "Why?" My mother's answer was, "For general principles!" On the weekends, my sister and I did all the chores: we cleaned the house, washed clothes, and shopped for groceries. If we forgot to buy something on the shopping list, my mother used to become very angry, fuss and yell, then send us back to the store to get it. One Saturday, when my sister went shopping for groceries, she saw some of her friends, talked to them for a while, and lost the money. Fear gripped my heart; I didn't know what was going to happen to us. Surprisingly, my mother was so upset by the loss of the money that she just cried and retreated to her bedroom.

Also in the mid-sixties, on the weekends, my mother's half-sisters started taking her out to bars and clubs at night. After my mother would take her bath, my sister and I helped her get dressed, and she would go out leaving my sister to babysit. While out partying, my mother used to call home to check on my sister and me. One time before my mother went out with her sisters, she noticed that there was some money missing in her wallet. She questioned my sister and me about the money. I had no idea about the money and my sister didn't say a word; therefore, my mother said, "When I come home, I want to see the money on the dining room table." Before my mother came home, she called my sister on the telephone to let her know that she was on her way home. Then my sister's crooked mind had a plan. She decided to tell my mother that I stole the money. She grabbed my pocketbook and placed the money in it.

Then when my mother returned home that evening, my sister told my mother she found the money in my pocketbook. My mother looked at me with such shock on her face, and yet I think she didn't believe my sister's story because she did not punish me for the crime. My sister did bad things like that and then told my mother I did it, or she just made up accusations to tell my mother. While my mother was hanging out with her sisters, she started making friends, a lot of friends. Her friends encouraged her to have fun. We spent more weekends in Atlantic City and New York for several years in the late sixties. Also, during the summer, my sister and I would spend two weeks in camp then go to Atlantic City or New York after camp. We were involved with fashion shows, dance, and music. Our summers were full of fun! However, in the late sixties, my junior high school years, my mother stopped sending my sister and me to camp and she stopped taking us to Atlantic City and New York.

For some reason, my mother retreated back to her bedroom; therefore, during the summer, my sister and I started socializing with the teens in the neighborhood. My mother allowed my sister to go to parties with her friends, but she had to take me along with her. After a while, my mother encouraged my sister to have parties at the house with her friends from the neighborhood and from school. Here is where the chaos started in the house again. My mother decided to have a clubhouse in our house, so the boys came to our house every weekend. Then it got to the point where the boys waited until my mother left for work in the morning so they could enter the house and play hooky from school. Teenage boys were in the house all the time. They ate food, smoked their cigarettes, and some drank alcohol. On Saturdays, the teenage boys hung out all day in the house smoking cigarettes, drinking alcohol, and playing cards in the dining room. The parties went on for a year until one of the boys was attacked by a gang member, which we didn't know existed, and he was placed in the hospital for stab wounds. Also, my sister decided to go to college and live in the dormitory.

My friends and I sat on my front steps for hours to listen to each other's idle conversation and laughed at each other's jokes while I braided the boys' hair. During my high school years on the weekends, after my sister moved out, I used to either go to a party or I used to have a party at my house. I was known for braiding hair and for having the best parties. This was around the time when my neighborhood started going down. In 1973, right before I graduated high school, it seemed as if Hell had opened its gates and unleashed a military of demonic spirits to infiltrate my neighborhood. We started hearing rumors about gang activity. We started hearing rumors about gang wars. Two gangs, the Drifts and the Coons, started fighting several blocks from where I lived, somewhere near 60th and Market Streets. We lost our sense of security and started locking our doors and windows. Some of the neighbors stayed in the house to isolate themselves.

My parent's house was robbed several times, so my mother put bars on our windows. Furthermore, now my neighborhood was under police surveillance, and a curfew ordinance was established. Everyone under the age of eighteen had to be in the house by ten o'clock or be arrested by the police. I stopped having parties because some of the gang's groupies crashed my party. They came in my house with beer and wine and my house became over crowded. My friends and I were intimidated by this; however, courage took over my heart and my mouth. I turned off the music and yelled, "Everybody, get out!" several times until everyone left, except my best girlfriend. I stopped having parties for fear that the members of one of the gangs would come and destroy my parent's house. Moreover, the Violent family, a divorced wife with four sons and their destructive friends and one daughter, moved into our neighborhood across the street from my house on the corner of Samson and Alden Streets. The two middle sons, Fear – member of the Drift gang, and Thief-member of the Coon gang, a year younger, were high school dropouts.

The youngest son, Friendly, who was the nice guy in the family, became friends with my group of friends. And the one daughter, Confused, dropped out of school in the seventh grade and couldn't decide which gang to join. I had no knowledge about these gangs until this family moved into my neighborhood. The girls in these gangs were known to be just as rough and tough as the guys were. They had a reputation for ganging up on people and beating them down to the ground. I remember my first encounter with some of these girls. One afternoon after arriving home from high school, as I inserted my key into the lock of the front door, Wanna-Be, my best girlfriend's brother, approached me and said, "Andrea! Unattractive told some of the Drift girls that you broke up with him. They're on their way over here to fight you." I said, "Okay!" After he briskly walked away, I opened the front door and noticed that nobody else was home at that time.

My heart pounded rapidly. Whenever I felt anxious and fearful, my mind seemed to become rational. My strategy was to keep my parent's house safe and to not let these girls know where I lived. Therefore, I put my books and my pocketbook in the house, locked the door, and hid my key under one of the chairs on the porch. Next, I walked up the street and sat down on a knee-high red brick wall in front of my neighbor's house and waited for them. I had no idea what was going to happened to me. I sat there and calmly waited for them to come. When about six of the Drift girls approached me in their brazen, arrogant manner, one of them, the darkest, short, skinny one in the group, said, "So. You know. Like, we heard that you broke up with Unattractive." As I straightened my back to maintain my composure, I calmly said, "Yes, I broke up with him." Another girl, the tall, thin light-skin one with black hair said, "Well, that's all we wanted to know." I said, "Okay." The tall one repeated, "Okay." Then they just walked away.

I walked back to my house, retrieved my key from under the chair on the porch, unlocked the front door, walked into the house, closed the front door and locked it, flopped on the couch and exhaled deeply. I felt relieved. I had no idea why these girls did not jump on me. Later that evening, Wanna-Be told me that these girls would have jumped me if it weren't for the man sitting there with me. He asked, "So who was this man sitting with you?" I responded, "I don't know." I said I don't know because as far as I knew, I was the only one sitting there. Today, as I write this account, I say, "Thank You Jesus!" Several weeks later, after that incident, one night my mother gave me permission to spend the night over my girlfriend's house. Again, somebody came to warn me that the Drift girls were waiting for me to come outside. My mother hearing the news told my sister, who was shorter and smaller than I, to walk me across the street and around the corner to my girlfriend's house.

While we walked, the gang of girls followed us. I heard one say, "Who is this?" Another one said, "That's her sister." These girls followed us to the end of the street then walked away. Amazing! They could have jumped my sister and me, but they didn't. Another encounter I had with these gangs was when I was almost raped. One night Confused and I were sitting outside on the front steps of her house talking. I used to talk to her like a big sister would, giving her advice, and I tried to convince her not to get involved with any of the gangs. While I was talking to her, Buffalo, a member of the Coon gang approached us looking for Confused's brother, Thief. When she went into the house to see if her brother was there, I noticed that Buffalo had shaved off all his hair.

I laughed and asked, "What did you do with your hair?" Without any warning, he grabbed my left arm and bent my little finger back until it became numb. He said, "Come on and I'll show you." While Buffalo was holding my finger and pulling me to the driveway that led to the back of the houses on Samson Street, without even knowing what I was saying, I talked endlessly trying to convince him to let me go. Without any response to what I was saying, he kept walking as if he was determined to carry out whatever was on his mind. After we had passed about five or six houses, I knew we were walking to the unlighted area at the end of the driveway. Then, suddenly, I heard somebody call my name. I swiftly turned my head towards the voice that sounded like the mother of one of my friends and responded, "Yes!" I saw a tall translucent figure standing on the third or fourth step from the top of thirteen steps to the back of the house. When I turned back to my hand, Buffalo was gone.

 Then I had this urge to go to the house where I saw the tall figure standing. I hesitated at first because I knew the family had gone out for the evening and could've been on their way home, but I went anyway. I quickly climbed up the steps. The back door that led to the kitchen was wide open. This was unusual because everybody in the neighborhood locked their doors and windows before leaving the house. As I apprehensively walked through the house from the kitchen to the living room, I noticed that all the lights were on and the front door was also wide open. I quickly walked out of the house then walked straight home and sat on my porch wondering what had just happened. For years I marveled over the incident, but I never told anyone. Another night, that same summer about several weeks later, a few guys came to my house wanting their hair braided. We were sitting outside on my front steps when a man stopped his car in front of my house and said, "Tonight we're recruiting and we want girls too!"

I was told that this man was a member of the Coon gang. This did not frighten me. In fact, about nine o'clock that night, after I finished braiding hair, all of us, about six of us, decided to walk to the corner of 58th and Samson streets. When we arrived, we came upon several of my other friends who were on their way to my house. While we were standing on the corner talking, out of nowhere, some guy appeared and started threatening one of my friends. I did not hear what the guy said, but I heard when my friend chuckled and said, "Common, man. Wha' chu talkin' about?" Then somebody else asked, "What did he say?" I turned around to see what was going on. The guy said again only this time with a loud voice, "I have a gun!" When he pointed the gun in the air and started shooting, one of the girls screamed and we all scattered running.

Because I was a little over weight at the end of my teen years, I was out of shape and not a good runner, but on this night, I was moving fast! In fact, to my amazement, I was literally moving very fast to the point that my feet were not touching the ground. Instead of watching where I was running to, I was busy watching how fast I was passing all of the other guys who were much taller and faster. It seemed as if I was in a vehicle moving about forty miles an hour because their faces were a blur. When I arrived on the corner of 58th and Chestnut Streets, I noticed that my feet were back on the ground and there were no cars travelling on Chestnut Street, which was usually busy. Moreover, it was quiet and I was the only one standing on that corner. However, I heard an audible voice say, "Go home!" So I did. After that summer, the influence of evil became extremely dense like a thick cloud of dark smoke in my neighborhood. By mid-1973, several of the neighbors had moved away.

One evening, after arriving home from my date with my high school boyfriend, who was from North Philadelphia, he noticed that there was something hanging from the tree in front on my house. We both discovered that the boys in the neighborhood, as a joke, hung a doll from the tree. That scared the boyfriend so much he decided not to visit me any longer. In 1974, after I graduated high school, my mother finally decided to move out of Philadelphia to South Jersey. We left that neighborhood, but I was haunted every night for about twenty years with dreams of being chased. From April 1976 to June 1977, I was employed by the United States Army. That didn't last too long for two reasons: my health and my street attitude; therefore, I was released. The summer of 1977, a girlfriend of mine and I decided to drive to Los Angeles, California. She wanted to become a Hollywood movie star, so we packed my car and drove four days across the country. What a beautiful experience!

The following year, 1978, while living in Los Angeles, a co-worker invited me to a Bible study. On the night of the Bible study, my co-worker's mother-in-law prayed over me. While praying over me, she started yelling, "It's starting to come out! It's coming out!" They quickly pushed me outside on the front porch. Then I heard a yell, and I noticed tears were coming from my eyes and yet I was not crying. When she let me back in the house, she started teaching me from the Bible. That Sunday, June 1978, I went to meet my co-worker and her mother-in-law in church. At the end of service, the pastor invited people to come and receive the Baptism in the Holy Spirit. I walked to the front of the sanctuary, the pastor prayed over all those who came forward, and then we were escorted out the side door to a garden area. It was a beautiful sunny summer afternoon.

In the garden area of the church grounds, there were chairs for us to sit with one of the members of the church. I don't remember the conversation I had with the woman, except I remember her slightly placing the fingertips of her right hand on my forehead. I closed my eyes and felt so comfortable and relaxed. I felt a tingle around my nose and mouth and I started speaking in an unknown language. The woman was amazed at my response. I heard her say, "Wow!" She let me speak for about a minute then she stopped me. This was my second known experience with God. Finally, it was time to leave. As everyone exited the building, I noticed that my co-worker and her mother in law were not in this church. I was at the wrong church, and yet as I write this, I realize that I was truly at the right place.

Later on that same day, as I was walking towards my apartment building in Inglewood, California, I met another woman who invited me to church. I became a member of a non-denominational Pentecostal church, in Inglewood, California and was water baptized. Since 1978, I have been attending church services. I came back home to South Jersey in 1980 and shared the Gospel with my family who all became born-again Christians. I now tell people about my born-again experience in 1961. It was the summer of 1973 while living in West Philadelphia, I was miraculously rescued, and it is only by the grace and power of God, my Heavenly Father, that I am alive today and able to tell my story.

THE DEVINE CONNECTION
Crossing the Bridge

It was a beautiful cool, sunny spring morning here in southern New Jersey. While waiting for the New Jersey Transit 403 bus to Philadelphia, I noticed that the wind was a little brisk and there were no insects flying around. It was the best time of the year. I can remember it clearly because something very significant happened to me that changed the course of my life.

The early summer session of 2007, I taught English Composition at Community College of Philadelphia in Pennsylvania. On the bus, one Friday morning on my way to work, I noticed a bee flying towards the ceiling. I decided to ignore it since it was flying high. This was brave of me because several years ago when a bee flew into my mother's house, I wasn't so brave. I quickly ran to the kitchen to grab a broom so that I could catch that bee and beat it to death. While I was swinging at it, the bee started buzzing and dodging the broom. The battle was on! I thought that if I ran in fear, the bee would chase and sting me, which made me determine to kill it. So in order to get the fear off of me, I yelled at the top of my voice, "You're dead! You are dead!" several times until I caught that bee and beat it to death. I was not going to run in fear of that bee.

Therefore, I decided this time, on the bus that Friday morning, to ignore the bee, especially since it was flying high, and I didn't think it would bother anybody. I turned my head away from it to look outside the bus window to view the trees and the different houses on this particular road and, at the same time, to listen to three men discussing a scripture from the Bible about the woman who hid leaven in three measures of meal. It was an interesting conversation. I overheard these men say that the leaven was compared to sin and the measures of meal represented the church or people in the church. They argued about how sin was creeping in to the church. One man said, "Look at the kind of music young people listen to." And the other man said, "What you call sin is not what other people would have called sin. Some people think that the Hip-Hop music young people listen to was ungodly, but from what I understand, there are some Christian Hip-Hop artists." I sort of agreed with him. The other man said in agreement, "I'm quite sure that some people in the church in the early 19th century did not like the faster pace hymnals that the mid-19th century church people started singing, and they probably had said that the modern music of that time was a sin and was ungodly."

I really wanted to join in the argument and express my point of view. When I had turned my head away from the window to see the man who made the statement about the Hip-Hop music, to my shocking surprise, the bee had landed on the back of the seat in front of my face. I jumped out of my seat and yelled, "There's a bee on the bus and I don't do well with bees! You know what I'm saying?!" When I yelled, the bee flew to the front of the bus just above the driver's head at his rear view mirror. I said, "Bus driver! It's flying near your rear view mirror. At your next stop, open the door and let it out!" At the next stop, the bus driver opened the door and the bee flew out. Before I sat down, I apologized to the other passengers for the sudden outburst. Some of them thanked me for alerting them. Soon after I sat down, I took a deep breath to calm myself.

It must have been about five minutes later, after everyone had settled down, when the man sitting across from me decided to initiate a conversation with me: "You sure did sound the alarm." I responded, "I guess I did. I'm glad it chased that bee off the bus." That began our conversation. He asked, "Are you on your way to work?" I responded, "Yes. I am." He continued, "I'm on my way to school." He told me that he is in the process of finishing a course in business at the Wharton School of the University of Pennsylvania. Then he continued the conversation to talk about politics and how he knew about certain events before they had happened. At that point, I slightly faded out of the conversation.

I really wasn't that interested in what he was saying because I was busy admiring how handsome he was. You see, several nights before, I dreamt I was walking across the Benjamin Franklin Bridge from Camden, New Jersey to Philadelphia, Pennsylvania. This bridge was wide with about four to six lanes. As I was walking, I felt as if I was lagging behind. Then Jesus extended his arm to me. When I connected my arm to His, I felt a warm sensation flood my being. I felt good all over, inside and out. While we walked together, I noticed there were gray looking clay models in the process of destroying cars on the bridge but were frozen in position as Jesus and I were walking pass them. I faded back into the conversation before the man on the bus could notice that I was hardly listening to him by asking, "How do you know all that information?"

With a slight smile on his face, he responded, "I read my books." I questioned, "What books?" He answered, "My Bible and other books pertaining to the Bible." To carry on the conversation, I asked, "Oh! Where do you fellowship?" I must have hit a *joy button* on this man because with a much bigger smile on his face, he leaned closer to me, and I felt some kind of connection when our eyes met. He told me the name of the church, the history of the church, and the location of the church, which was in walking distance from where I live. All this information just flowed out of his mouth like a running faucet. His smile and his enthusiasm about his church prompted me to ask him, "Do me a favor and write the name and phone number of the church for me?" as I handed him a pen and a piece of paper. When he gave me back the paper, I noticed he didn't just give me the name of the church; he also gave me his name. When it came time for him to exit the bus, he said, "Sister? . . . Sister?" I said, "Oh!" and told him my name. Then he bid me a good day.

After he left the bus, all I could say to myself was "Wow!" That was the only expression I could think of. I was truly amazed and full of wonder: "Could he be Mr. Right?" Later that evening on my way home, as I rode on the bus, my mind drifted to the events of that morning: the perfect, sunny, no-insect morning; the bee on the bus when I didn't see any other bugs flying that morning; the gentleman – very handsome; and then the conversation. "Wow!" Again, that was the only expression I could think of. After I arrived home from work, I sat on my couch and again pondered on the events of the day. And again, I had the same response, "Wow! Could he be Mr. Right? I live in walking distance from the church." And on that note, I decided to visit the church that Sunday.

The Devine Connection:
The Bridge

Several years before this meeting on the bus, I did a study on John 17: 20 – 23 (NIV). Jesus Prays for All Believers:

"My prayer is not for them alone. I pray also for those who will believe in Me through their message, that all of them may be one, Father, just as You are in Me and I am in You. May they also be in Us so that the world may believe that You have sent Me. I have given them the glory that You gave me, that they may be one as we are one— I in them and You in Me—so that they may be brought to complete unity. Then the world will know that You sent Me and have loved them even as You have loved Me."

Several nights later, I dreamt that it was the last evening of the women's weekend retreat. All of the women were told to pray together in the one room.

While we were all in prayer, a woman came into the prayer room to select some of the women one by one and urged them to follow her out of the prayer room making them feel special. Each one of those women chose one or several other women to follow them. The woman who selected the women out of the prayer room had a special room for them to gather in. The chosen women were placed in a room across the hall from the special room. Then there were the others who stayed in the main room. Now this makes three groups of women. I was chosen by one of the selected women to follow her out of the main room. Without thinking, I followed the woman who chose me. Then I was led to the room designated for the chosen, which was across the hall from the special room. The women in this room fell asleep, so I decided to go across the hall to the special room thinking that these women were in prayer.

When I walked into the room, I noticed there was a television set that was on and the women were huddled in a group. It looked as if they were playing a card game. I became frustrated and decided to leave that room. When I walked outside, I saw a few other women in the stairwell talking, but these women were not a part of the prayer group; therefore, I returned to the room designated for the chosen women. But they were still sleeping. Disappointed with their lack of concern with following the instructions, I walked back across the hall and discovered that all the selected women were gone. I asked the woman sitting on the window's ledge while smoking a cigarette, who pulled the women out of the prayer room, "Where did they go?" She said, "They went to a homeless shelter to feed the poor." For some reason I did not believe her, so I just walked away. I looked at my watch and saw that I had over stayed my time and decided to pack my things and go home.

That morning, I asked the Holy Spirit for the explanation of the dream. In the dream, the women were all in one room, the prayer room, praying as they were instructed to do. These women in the dream represented the Body of Christ. There was a spirit of unity in that room that was powerful. Then an enemy, represented by the woman who entered the room to select and urge a few women to follow her, was sent to divide the women and rob them of the gift of unity. The enemy, sitting on the window's ledge and smoking a cigarette at the end of the dream, accomplished her deed of divide and conquer and was satisfied. The devil uses the weaknesses in our personalities to keep us divided, hence denominational churches. The selected women and their chosen represent all of us who feel either superior or inferior, which are our weaknesses. The devil thinks that if he can continue to divide us, we will never experience the gift of unity that Jesus prayed to the Father to give us in John 17: 20-23: "... that they may be one as we are one— I in them and You in Me—so that they may be brought to complete unity."

I share this dream because I was a member of an Assemblies of God church for about twenty-five years. After my mother passed, I moved out of her house and out of the area to a new location. Now, I needed to find a new place of worship; therefore, I looked forward to going to this Deliverance church that Sunday morning for the service, and of course, to see if I would have any further interest with the gentleman who I met on the bus that Friday morning. When I arrived at the location of the church, to my amazement it was a small building with one front door. It was a small community church, similar to what I had seen in a movie. When I walked into the building, I noticed a small congregation of people singing joyfully. One by one they turned to see who came in the door as I was greeted by the ushers, who handed me a bulletin and led me to a seat. I was not used to such a small church and congregation; however, I knew that God led me to this place for His purpose. Two weeks went by when I decided to join this congregation. I was enthused about the fact that we spoke the same faith language and the people seemed to be friendly and united.

Before that Wednesday night service, I had to meet with the pastors in one of the back rooms. The pastor's wife, who is also a pastor, informed me and *emphasized* the fact that they were a

Deliverance church and that I would need to get to know how *they* do things in the church. I said that was fine; I am always willing to learn. The meeting went well. At the end of the meeting we shook hands and smiled at each other. Then I left the room to join the congregation in the sanctuary for the duration of prayer time. Also, that same night, there was a friendly couple in the church who befriended me and noticed that I did not have a car, so they decided to give me rides home after service. I was happy about that because at that time, I was walking to and from church. That Sunday, summer of 2007, I received the right hand of fellowship and officially became a member of the church. Oh, by the way, the man on the bus was there, but after a while, he started working a retail job and had to work on Sundays.

Well, that Wednesday night, the pastor announced that he had just finished a lesson on "protocol". So I questioned, "What is "Protocol?" He slightly smiled and said, "Oh, you'll learn!" Then one of the congregants said, "It has to do with leadership and respecting leadership." I just smiled and thought, "Okay." As the evening went on, I learned through the teaching about protocol and it seemed as if the pastor had to flex his muscles in the church to let everybody know who the boss is. That's when I started becoming a little leery. I had been a member of the Assemblies of God for about twenty-five years before I moved out of the area, and I had been visiting other churches in search of a home church, but I had never been in a place where leadership had to flex his muscles and dominate the congregation. However, I stayed at this church because I remembered the dream about the bridge and the bus ride.

About several months went by when the pastor's wife asked me to meet with her because one Wednesday evening after service,

I told her, "I am not a pew warmer. I like to work in ministry." At the meeting, we talked about my church work and my career in education. She asked me if I wanted to be one of the Mothers in the church. I slowly emphasized, "No!" I'm not sure, but I think I insulted her when I said, "No." She became a little indignant while explaining to me the role of the Mothers in the church. Then I asked her, "Where was this in the Bible?" Again, being a little indignant, "There are scriptures in the Bible that talks about the Mothers in the church." After I humbly bowed out of that conversation by changing the subject, we ended our conversation when she told me she and the pastor will let me know what God has called me to do in the church. I left that little room questioning, "What is God going to tell them?"

At the end of the year, the pastor's wife asked me to help with the children's ministry. She said, "You're not ready to teach the adult class." I thought that statement was strange because I told her that I taught an adult Bible study group under the leadership of one of the deacons from the Assemblies of God church. But, I just dismissed the thought. The Mother over the children's ministry was in the process of preparing the children for their Christmas play. While sitting in the classroom among the children, I noticed there was some hostility in the air among the adults. I decided that was not going to deter me from working in the church. While attending the Assemblies of God church, I worked almost all of the children's ministries and enjoyed it. However, I noticed that this Mother was not pleased with me being called to work with her. Most of the time I sat and did nothing, but when she needed a helping hand with the children, she definitely gave me her orders.

About three weeks before the play, one Sunday morning, the pastor's wife asked me in front of the congregation to help with Sunday school because they were still in the process of preparing for the play. Envy gripped the heart of the wife of the friendly couple. She did not like the fact that the pastor's wife had called on me to help. The wife said, "I'm going to miss you." I just smiled at her as I got up to go the children's classroom. Most of the time in the classroom, I sat and watched the children rehearsed their parts. Then after Sunday school, I helped with getting the children to quietly line up so we all could go back into the sanctuary. When I returned to my seat in the sanctuary, the wife of the friendly couple asked me to join her for lunch after service. I smiled and said, "Yes, thanks!" not knowing that it was a set up. We had a good time laughing and talking at the diner while sharing lunch.

The Devine Connection:
The Gray Figures ~ The Battles

Later in that week, one evening, I received a phone call from somebody fussing at me for saying something bad about somebody in the church. At first I was shocked that somebody from this church was calling me and fussing in my ear. I yelled, "Who is this?" She kept fussing about me saying something bad about somebody in the church. I sensed anger rising up in me and responded back, "I don't know anybody in the church!" several times. Next thing I knew she hung up. Well, I have a cell phone, so I decided to call to see who had called me. And, of course, nobody answered the phone. That Wednesday afternoon, the pastor's wife told the secretary of the church to call and ask me to come to a meeting with her before service. When I went to this meeting in one of the back rooms of the sanctuary, I noticed that the pastor's wife and two board members were sitting in the room on one side with a table in front of them and they had a chair sitting and waiting for me to sit on the other side of the table. After the pastor's wife and one of the board members so calmly and softly spewed out their accusations at me, I calmly asked the panel of judges, "Who is my accuser and what did I say, exactly?"

The Mother, who called me on the phone fussing with her accusation, didn't say much, but the look on her red face was if she was about to burst in anger. The other board member and the pastor's wife were a little evasive, but through what they did say, I discovered that the wife of the friendly couple told the pastors that I said bad things about the pastors. I denied, "I have not said anything bad about anybody in this church because I don't know anybody in the church." They warned me that most of the members of the church were family, so if I say something about somebody, it will get back to that person. Then, to knock the devil out of the situation, I said, "If I don't like what's being preached in this church, I could just go to another church!" There was a pause as if they were lost for words; therefore, the meeting ended with them warning me to watch what I say. After a cordial salutation, I exited the room. As I walked through the hall, I noticed that the wife of the friendly couple was sitting in a chair in the nursery room with her husband standing next to her. I was tempted to say something, but I just kept on walking. I entered the sanctuary and joined the others in prayer.

Not too long after I sat down in the sanctuary, the friendly couple entered the sanctuary and left the church. At the end of service that Wednesday night, the pastor's wife told me that the friendly couple said, "As long as she's here, we're not coming back." I said in my mind, "Well okay!" The end of that year came, and the children's Christmas play was nice. This was the first year of my membership. What an experience! That incident tainted my relationships with the members. They were kind as far as giving me rides to and from church, but no real friendships developed with them. For three years, I went to Bible Study on Wednesday nights, I went to the special services on Friday nights, and church service on Sundays. During the summer there were the picnics and trips to Wildwood, New Jersey, and there were the holiday gatherings with plenty of food, but there was no developed relationships, no real fellowship.

In October 2009, one Wednesday night at the end of service, the pastor announced to the congregation that he was going on a fast and invited the congregation to go on a fast with him. He gave some instructions: don't eat any food until after three o'clock in the afternoon and pray for an hour each day. He also said that the fast would last until January 2010, giving God the first fruits of the year. I was enthused about this because I was also praying for healing and an increase in my income. In 2007, I was diagnosed with End Stage Renal Disease, meaning my kidneys were no longer functioning. Because I was on dialysis, I asked the Father, "Since I can't fast on food, what could I fast on?" He said, "TV and Internet games." This fast was only to last up until the first of the year, January 2010; however, God kept me on the fast. While on this fast, I played praise and worship music and prayed while lying on the floor in my bedroom. After a while, the Lord instructed me to power walk, pacing back and forth in my apartment while praying. I continued this fast and prayer through the year.

Later on in the year, for some reason, the rides to and from church stopped. They didn't seem to have room in their cars. I really didn't think about it; I just walked. As I said before, the church was in walking distance from my home. One Wednesday night after service, the pastor's wife called me to the front and asked, "Do you need a ride home?" I said, "No, but that's okay; I'll walk. Then she asked me if I knew why nobody wanted to take me home or pick me up for church. Clueless, I said, "No, but that's okay." She said, "Maybe you need to find out. I want you to meet with the pastor before next Wednesday night's service." I said, "Okay;" however, I sensed something bad was about to happen. I already had one negative meeting in that back room.

That following Wednesday night, the meeting was cancelled; therefore, I had to wait for the secretary to let me know when the pastors would be available. So I waited. The following Sunday, Passover Sunday, during offering time at the opening of the service, I cheerfully stuffed an envelope with a check and placed it in the offering bucket marked "Pastor's Love Offering" with the words "Encouragement and Increase/Passover Seed" written on the check. The service that Sunday was enlightening; the anointing of God moved all of us. After service, I was ready to walk home when the secretary/usher came to me and said that the pastor wanted to meet with me in the back room. Strange. I sensed fear as I walked through the small sanctuary, down the short hallway, and into the back room. When I got there, I was surprised that this time the pastor, and not the pastor's wife, was in the room. The pastor's daughter also entered the room and we both sat across from him. After his daughter closed the door and sat, he said with a loud, stern voice, "The next time I hear that you said one more poison thing out of your mouth, I'm gonna *kick* you out of this church!" And boy did he emphasize the word "kick". I said nothing as sternly directed by him before the threat.

I was in shock! I looked at him as if to question, "What are you talking about?" He read my expression and responded with a loud voice of anger, "Don't act as if you don't know what I'm talking about!" As he stood up and walked towards the door to open it, the fear inside me turned to intense anger. I was practically on his heels behind him ready to run out the door when he turned and blurted out something else about he had called another church where I had visited, as if that pastor had said something bad about me, but at that time I was extremely angry that I didn't hear much of what he said. Because I was a new member, the pastors automatically believed the accusations that were coming from the unknown accuser. As soon as he opened the door and began to walk out, I stomped out of that room, stomped down the hall, and stomped all the way home in a fit. When I arrived home, I exploded into the mother of all tantrums. As a child, I used to throw tantrums, but this time, it was the biggest ever. I told God, "I don't care if I go to hell, I hate that man! Nobody talks to me like that! Nobody!"

I paced back and forth in my apartment for several hours in anger. I washed my face, made my meals for the week, straightened up my apartment. I fussed at God the whole time not realizing I had given place to a demon spirit. I really couldn't express the hurt I felt until my sister called me on the phone. Then I cried and cried. I was emotionally wounded. The anger and unrest lasted for a couple of days. That Monday night, the pastor's wife called me to find out why I left the church in a hurry. I told her, "The pastor yelled at me and threatened to kick me out of the church; therefore, it was better for me to leave the church and not disrespect the pastor." At first she commended me for not disrespecting the pastor; then she denied that the pastor yelled at me. I was ready to go through the phone at her, but I restrained myself.

Then she said, "Well, you keep saying things." Those words fueled my anger, but again I restrained myself when I responded, "What things am I saying and who are my accusers?" Again, just as the first meeting with her, there was that pause in the phone and then the warning, "Just watch what you say to people." Exasperated, I thought, "Whatever!" We ended the conversation on a positive note and bid each other a good night. Tuesday night I talked to the Lord about it, and He healed me so that I was able to sleep in peace. This was the second incident. What I had discovered from that telephone call was that several of the congregants who were giving me rides to church were lying to the pastors telling them that I was saying things that contradicted what was being taught, as if to persuade them to not believe what was being taught. Moreover, I discovered that the people in this very small congregation did not fellowship with one another and there were a few who definitely did not like each other. I discovered that the friendly looking people I saw on the first day I walked in the building were not that friendly and were not as *united* as I thought; therefore, I could not fellowship with anybody at this church. This takes me back to the message God gave me about the lack of unity in the Body of Christ.

The Devine Connection:
Light Expels the Darkness

While on dialysis, there were certain foods I could not eat and I had to limit my fluid intake. It was summertime and summer fruits were in season. I became frustrated because I could not eat any fresh fruit; therefore, I figured I'd eat can fruit, instead of fresh fruit. Well of course, if I can't eat fresh fruit, why did I think I could eat can fruit that was soaked in sugar water? One evening, when I opened a can of peaches and dumped them into a bowl, using a fork, I picked up a slice of peach, opened my mouth, and right before I put a slice of peach in my mouth, I heard the Lord say, "Throw it away." Holding the slice of peach on the fork near my face I yelled, "What?" He softly repeated Himself, "Throw it away." I responded, "You've got to me kidding me! Why?" He calmly responded, "Too much fluid." He then moved my feet to the sink to dump the bowl of peaches. So I threw a tantrum and decided to take the bowl of peaches out to the dumpster and *throw* it away.

Another evening, while power walking and praying in my apartment, I accidently bumped my leg several times on the edge of my glass coffee table. When anger exploded on the inside of me I yelled at the top of my voice, "What the heck?" Then a thought popped in my mind, "Break the coffee table and throw it out my front window." I knew not to do that. It was too extreme and that's not me. Feeling intensely angered as I walked, I said, "I am so freaking angry!" several times. As I said earlier, I gave place to a demon spirit when I became extremely angry with the pastor of this particular church and said to God, "I don't care if I go to hell, I hate that man!" after he had reprimanded me and threatened to kick me out of his church. Therefore, the littlest things were making me angry. I asked God what was wrong with me. He said, "You have an anger problem." I really didn't know what to say or do at that point but to ask the Father to forgive me for being so angry.

Starting in December 2010 on Wednesday nights, the pastors decided to teach an exhaustive study, a series of lessons, about the curse and demon spirits called "Getting From Under the Curse." The lesson was about how some born-again believers needed deliverance. One particular Wednesday night, he said, "Deliverance is not for the unbeliever; deliverance is for the believer." In the first lesson, "Witchcraft", he said that rebellion is the sin of witchcraft and stubbornness is a form of idolatry, trusting in ourselves more than trusting in God. While listening, I learned that these sins give place to the curse in our lives. Also, I learned that an undisciplined thought life gives place to the curse. Unforgiveness and fears bring about the curse in our lives. Sin opens the door to the curse and repentance closes it. This was all news to me so I took plenty of notes to reflect on later.

On Sundays, at the end of service, the pastor invited people to come to the front of the sanctuary for prayer. While there was loud music playing in the background, I watched how the pastor smeared oil on the people's foreheads, placed his hand on top of their heads and prayed over them casting out spirits. While the pastor prayed, the ushers had to hold a trash bucket in front of some of them with plenty of paper towels. I guess they had to vomit. Some people fell to the floor; however, this one man, or say the spirit in him, resisted and was trying to pull away so the ushers had to hold him as the pastor prayed. In June 2011, one Sunday morning at the end of service, I decided to go up for prayer.

As I stood in line, I felt like a little girl in the waiting room of the doctor's office not knowing what was going to happened to me. Was I going to convulse and vomit like a few others or fall out? When it was my turn, he smeared my forehead with oil and put his hand on my head and prayed. I was told that I was resisting and was pushed to the floor. While lying on the floor, a voice said, "Get me up off this floor!" So I knew for certainty I needed help.

The Devine Connection:
The Connection

The battle was on. I needed deliverance. Every night at nine o'clock, I began my power walk in my apartment, pacing from the back to the front, and my prayer time. At first I sensed fear, but knowing that fear is a demon spirit, I knew I had to continue praying. I called on Jesus for deliverance. In James 5: 16, James says, "The effectual fervent prayer of a righteous person avails much." At night each week, I became more and more aggressive against the spirits of rebellion, stubborn, fear, and anger by praying certain scriptures from the Bible for healing, salvation, deliverance, and who I am in Christ Jesus, along with binding the forces of Satan. Every night during my prayer time, I power walked in my apartment, prayed in the spirit, and bind those spirits out of my life. I called out the spirit of anger out of my body, out of my life. I told it who I am in Christ Jesus and what I know from the WORD of God!

Almost two years later, by June 2011, I'm still fasting as well as praying. One Wednesday night Bible study, the pastors taught about casting out spirits and the different kinds of sins and how they relate to different kinds of spirits. Again, I thought of rebellion, stubborn, fear, and anger. That Wednesday evening after service, I became more determined to get those spirits out of my body, out of my life. I paced back and forth in my apartment as fast as I could while saying, "Get out! Get out of my life in the name of Jesus!" I expressed who I am in Christ Jesus and all that I have in Him. I used the power and authority that God has given every believer, the name of Jesus, and the WORD of God. I did this for hours. Also, I am baptized in the ♥Holy Spirit♥ and speak in tongues according to Acts chapter two.

I am familiar with how my prayer language sounds; however, this night a strange language with much force welled up within me and it seemed there was an argument going on. I yelled in my understanding, "There's no argument! Get out! The blood of Jesus is against you!" Finally, that evil presence popped out of my nostril and ran. There were a few cats outside that didn't even want that spirit in them. I heard them scream and growl. Hallelujah! Thank You, Jesus! I am free! I am delivered from that demon spirit of anger and rebellion. Not only that, I have not had any more sinus problems since.

As I continued going to this church, God's purpose became clear to me why He led me to this Deliverance church and I am thankful for the work He has done in me, but I still was not satisfied and felt as if these pastors would not be good for me. In fact, one last incident occurred while I was waiting on God to make my move to leave this church. One Sunday morning in July, the pastors' neighbor and his son came to visit the church. Now this congregation was very small so sometimes I would spread my bag, my Bible, and my coat on the pew if nobody was going to sit with me. This one Sunday, the usher escorted the pastors' neighbor to the pew where I was sitting. The usher wanted me to get up and let the man slide in and sit; however, some weeks prior, I was told by the head usher that the pastor wanted the men to sit on the first seat of the pew or on the outside and for me to slide over. Following the instructions of the head usher, I gathered up my things and slid over so that the man and his son could sit. Not only that, I apologized to the man for having to wait. He said, "That's okay."

That Wednesday night, the pastor's lecture, instead of teaching, was about how we were to handle ourselves when company comes to the house for a visit. He talked about his neighbor who came to visit and how there were only a few seats, which was a good thing because the house was usually half full. The whole time he was talking, several times I heard in my mind, "He's talking about you." I said, "No he is not!" thinking maybe somebody else wouldn't move to let the neighbor and his son sit, so the usher brought them to where I was sitting. I don't remember the question he asked, but I raised my hand to answer it. He proceeded to accuse me of "hogging" a seat. He thought that I did not want his neighbor to sit next to me and reprimanded me in front of the congregation who all laughed and thought it was funny. After service, I went to the front of the sanctuary to speak with the pastor: "I wasn't "hogging" the seat! I was gathering my things so I could slide over!" He said, "Well, you didn't move fast enough." While I was still trying to defend myself, the Mother of the church used her body to shield the pastor as if I was going to commit a crime.

As I walked away from the front of the sanctuary, one of the other board members following me said, "Well, why don't you go back to your own church?" That was it for me. That was my cue to walk out of that building, walk home, and don't return. About a week and a half later, I sent the pastors a pleasant e-mail thanking them for their prayers and support and how God has truly blessed my soul and blessed me financially. They told the secretary to call me to set up an appointment. When she called, she said, "The pastors said they will meet with you on Wednesday before service." I said, "No thank you." She said, "Well, how about on Sunday after service?" I said, No thank you." She said, "You're not coming back to the church?" I said, "No."

There were a number of incidents such as these that had happened to me at this church, too many to name and too petty. When I cried out to God, He answered me and introduced me to an evangelist from another church through my voice instructor of the Lawnside Music Studio. In the same month, July 2011, when one of the board members said, "Why don't you go back to your own church," the evangelist invited me to a Family and Friends Day at the church where she is a member. In August 2011, she invited me to their church picnic. In September, I became a member of a Church of God in Christ in Lawnside, New Jersey. And now, I am a member of a non-denominational Pentecostal Christian center. My soul is satisfied! I learned something from this experience. Faith comes by hearing the WORD of God. Just as a farmer plants seed in the ground, the Word of Deliverance was planted in my heart. When the pastor smeared my forehead with oil and prayed for deliverance, I thought nothing happened because there was no immediate outward change; however, there was an immediate inward change. I was moved by the WORD of God to take action.

And by closely observing the pastors and how they prayed for others, I knew I had to perform the same kind of prayers. Also,

I understood why God kept me on that fast. In Matthew 7: 21, Matthew says, "Howbeit this kind goeth not out but by prayer and fasting." Moreover, the ♥Holy Spirit of God♥ revealed to me the interpretation of the dream. The dream about me walking across the Benjamin Franklin Bridge from Camden, New Jersey to Philadelphia, Pennsylvania was about me leaving the Assemblies of God. The wide bridge was the Deliverance church. The gray looking clay models in the process of destroying the cars on the bridge but were frozen in position were symbols of the battles that I had to go through. Walking alone on the bridge was the fact that I felt as if I had to take care of the deliverance process by myself because I felt as if the pastor couldn't help me. The burden of feeling as if I was lagging behind in the dream was that the process of deliverance seemed overwhelming. That's when I called on Jesus.

In the dream, He extended His arm to me. When I connected my arm to his, I felt a warm sensation flood my being. I felt good all over, inside and out. That was the divine connection and my deliverance. And now I am on the other side of the bridge: from Assemblies of God, crossing the bridge through the Deliverance Church to the Church of God in Christ. The farmer plants seed in the ground and God plants the seed of His WORD in our hearts. This poem is called "Occupation"

Inspiration Motivation Vegetation Plantation Cultivation Immersion
Celebration Anticipation Frustration Exasperation Immersion
Cultivation Confirmation Examination Immersion
Anticipation Frustration Examination Germination
Protrusion Excitation Annunciation Congregation Accumulation
Congratulation Celebration Jubilation Adoration Glorification.

My Calling
A Nun In The Protestant Church

Isaiah 54:5 King James Version (KJV) says, "For thy Maker is thine Husband; the LORD of hosts is His name; and thy Redeemer the Holy One of Israel; The God of the Whole Earth shall He be called." The Catholic Church for centuries has had orders of priest, eunuchs, and nuns where some of the people in that denomination decide to dedicate their lives to God and the ministry. According to Dictionary.com, a nun is a woman who is a member of a religious order, especially one bound by vows of chastity and obedience. And chastity is the abstention from sexual intercourse; virginity or celibacy: a vow of chastity. The Protestant churches have looked at those people as if they were doing a religious duty in that particular religion; however, what we don't want to recognize is that what the Catholic Church is doing is scripturally correct in that God does call some people not to marry. In Matthew 19:11-13 New International Version (NIV), "Jesus replied, 'Not everyone can accept this word, but only those to whom it has been given. For there are eunuchs who were born that way, and there are eunuchs who have been made eunuchs by others—and there are those who choose to live like eunuchs for the sake of the kingdom of heaven. The one who can accept this should accept it.'" I struggled

with this for years because I was one of the ones called of God not to marry, yet I am in the Protestant Church where this is not recognized, taught, or accepted. In some churches, they call it "the gift of celibacy" and in other churches, it's just not recognized at all. I'm sharing my story on this in hoping that many will read it and the burden of getting married will be lifted off the shoulders of single people who are called of God not to marry.

No sooner after my father passed in December 1960, I accepted Jesus as my Savior in 1961 at six years old while sitting in my Sunday school class. It was in the summer of 1963, when my mother continued taking one day trips to meet family in Atlantic City, NJ. While riding in the back seat of my mother's light blue 1956 Chevy Impala, after we had crossed the Ben Franklin Bridge into Camden, New Jersey from Philadelphia, Pennsylvania, I heard these words, "You're getting married." At the time I heard those words, I was only eight years old; therefore, I kept those words to myself and allowed them to settle deep into my subconscious. During my teen years, I didn't think about what I had heard that day, except that I seriously wanted a boyfriend. Years later, in the summer of 1977, after I was dismissed out of the Army, twenty-two years old at the time, I was ready to leave home again. My girlfriend and I decided to drive to Los Angeles, California because she wanted to be a Hollywood movie star; therefore, we packed my car with clothes and food and drove four days across the country. The following year, 1978, while living in Los Angeles, a co-worker invited me to a Bible study. She and her mother-in-law prayed over me and started teaching me from the Bible about Salvation. That Sunday in June, I went to meet my co-worker and her mother-in-law in church.

My Calling

I arrived a little after service started; therefore, since there were many people in the congregation, I couldn't see if my co-worker and her mother-in-law were there. I walked down the center aisle to a seat as close to the front as I could get. I don't recall the message that was preached that day; however, I do remember the pastor giving the invitation at the end of service to come and receive the Baptism in the Holy Ghost. I slowly stood to my feet and walked to the front of the sanctuary, along with others who accepted the invitation. The pastor said a few words, prayed over us, and then gave us direction to follow the altar workers. The altar workers escorted us out a side door to a garden area. The sun shone brightly that day. There were chairs set in small groups of two and three. I sat one-on-one with one of the altar workers. I don't recall exactly what she said, but I do remember she let me know that she was going to place her hand on my head and for me to begin to pray.

Without even questioning, I submitted to her instructions. I closed my eyes and lifted my head as she placed the tip of her fingers on my forehead. Instantly, I began to speak in a language other than English as the Holy Spirit gave me the utterance. That Sunday, I was baptized in the Holy Ghost with the evidence of speaking in another language (tongues). After prayer, I was given a few pamphlets and was escorted back into the sanctuary only to discover I was at the wrong church. My co-worker and her mother-in-law were at another church. However, as I sit and recall this day, thank God I was at the wrong church and in the center of His will for me that day. Later on that same day, on my way home from church, I met another woman, who lived across the street from where I lived, who also invited me to church. At the age of twenty-four, I became a member of a non-denominational Christian Center in Los Angeles, California and was water baptized. This was in the late seventies during the time when the "Faith Movement" became popular.

Some people hated "The Faith Movement" as it was titled during that time and some people loved it and followed it. This was my first time going to church since I was seven years old, so I didn't have an opinion of it either way. I was just glad to know "Therefore if any man be in Christ, he is a new creature: old things are passed away; behold, all things are become new" (2 Corinthians 5: 17). That meant to me that a certain part of my life was over. Several other scripture verses also became a part of my foundational teaching: Mark 11: 22-24 (NKJV):

So Jesus answered and said to them, "Have faith in God. For assuredly, I say to you, whoever says to this mountain, 'Be removed and be cast into the sea,' and does not doubt in his heart, but believes that those things he says will be done, he will have whatever he says. Therefore I say to you, whatever things you ask when you pray, believe that you receive *them,* and you will have *them.*

And, in Psalms 37:4, the Lord says "Delight yourself in the Lord and He will give you the desires of your heart." I settled my whole life into those verses of scripture, along with a whole list of other verses, I thought would change my life so that I could have whatever I wanted.

What was missing in that teaching was I John 5: 14: "And this is the confidence that we have in Him that if we ask any thing ACCORDING TO HIS WILL, He heareth us." This is where I stumbled because at that time, I did not know God's will/calling for my life. Moreover, I met single men and women who enjoyed

My Calling

going to church. A small group of us socialized together several times a week. This one woman and I moved into this big house where we rented our separate bedrooms, but we had access to the whole house as long as we took care of the house and the owner of the house, who was a ninety-four year old woman who was bed-ridden and weak after having been very sick. Before she passed, she accepted Jesus as her Savior. After she went Home to be with the Lord, her son told the other woman and me that we could stay in the house and continue to rent our rooms until the estate was settled, but the other woman decided to leave. Since I decided to stay in that big house, I asked the son if I could get other women to rent the other rooms, and he agreed. Two other women from my circle of single friends moved into the house. We were happy to be in that house together.

    The three of us shared in prayer and Bible study. We shared in household chores. We took turns in cooking dinner and shared conversation during dinner: a true family of friends. Therefore, I started inviting other single people to come to the house for Bible study and prayer. Then Desperation crept into our little circle of fellowship. The other two women in the house were in agony. I used to hear them crying in their bedrooms behind closed doors about some of the men in our circle of fellowship they wanted to marry. So, of course, influenced by their behavior, I started praying about getting married as well. That was when the words I heard when I was eight years old floated up from my subconscious and I recognized the voice of God in me from way back in 1963. As we were praying, and they were crying, the one woman looked at me and said, "Drea, the Lord told me to tell you to wait!" I was shocked and lost for words; however, thinking that those words came from God, all I did was walk away and retreated to my bedroom.

Several weeks later, Jesus began courting me. As I was standing in the kitchen at the sink washing dishes, a soft breeze swept across my right cheek. I looked and the kitchen window was closed. Then I heard Him say to me, "What would you like in a husband? Make a list." So I followed the instructions in Habakkuk 2:2, which says, "And the Lord answered me, and said, 'Write the vision, and make it plain upon tables, that he may run that readeth it. For the vision is yet for an appointed time, but at the end it shall speak, and not lie: though it tarry, wait for it; because it will surely come, it will not tarry." I developed my imagination and a list in my journal of all the qualities I desired for a husband from his spirit, to his soul, to his physical body, his family, and his occupation. This truly handsome man was going to be my dream-come-true. From that time on, I waited on God to bring this man into my life. I used scripture verses to pray.

I diligently and consistently prayed everyday imagining how my whole life would be with my new family. For some reason, at that time, some people thought that God's highest calling was to be married, so of course I was influenced to think the same way. You see, as a teenager, I suffered rejection. Yes, I had a few friends; however, none of the boys in the neighborhood wanted me for a girlfriend. I was teased, bullied, and even mistreated by a few family members. So, I just knew that now since I learned in church that God was going to give me my heart's desire, I went to the extreme with planning out the rest of my life, the sweet life I thought I would enjoy since I did not like my life growing up. Well, two years had gone by and it was time to leave Los Angeles and return home to

My Calling

New Jersey. In December 1980, I was on the plane crying feeling disappointed because I thought I was going to meet and marry the man of my dreams. It seemed as if all of the single people I socialized with found someone to date and marry, except for a small few, and I was included in the small few list. When I arrived home, I started going to church services with my mother at a deliverance church on north Broad Street in Philadelphia, Pennsylvania.

However, it wasn't until we left that church and started going to an Assemblies of God church in Mt. Ephraim, New Jersey that I started being seduced by Desperation. This church was filled with families. From the oldest to the youngest, somebody was connected to somebody and they were all happy together. I have heard some people say that the traditional family was becoming extinct; however, plenty do still exist and this church was full of them. I wanted to be a part of this to the point that Desperation brought in Envy. I wrote in my journal, "WAIT = a four letter word I hate". I craved to be married to the point that I had dreams of being married with children. One day during my lunch break on my job, I laid my head on my desk to rest. I fell asleep and dreamt that I was moving into a house where one part was still under construction. I had two little girls with me and I was placing a blue shirt and pants in the bottom drawer of a dresser. This signified that I was married and had three children. The two girls were twins, Candace and Christine. I said to the girls, "We're not really together yet, but some day we will really be together." One of the girls just stood and looked at me as if in shock and the other one was upset that we were not really together. I tried to console her in the dream then I awakened. You talk about deception!

I craved after marriage to the point that I cried out to God just like my two roommates in California, even though there was not a single man around that I was truly attracted to and none were attracted to me. Some married women said that the reason I still was not married was that I wasn't making myself available and that my standards were too high. These women had their reasons but none were true. I cried and craved so much to meet this man of my dreams and to get married that the Holy Spirit had to rebuke me. It was then I realized the evil influence that was over me. In my journal, I titled this entry "ENVY" and wrote,

"Wait brought this to my attention and helped me get rid of Longing. Longing distorts and is not of God. It distracts and can cause me to go crazy. I'm free of that and I will not give place to it again. But, I still have desires: a desire to be healthy and physically fit, to be happily married to the man of my dreams, and to work in ministry with him."

Several years went by when my mother and I left the Assemblies of God church for a while and started fellowshipping at another non-denominational church. Since living at home and fellowshipping with Single's Ministries, I felt led by the Holy Spirit to become head of the Single's Ministry at this church. Then this small singles fellowship made friends and joined in with another large group of singles from another church. On Tuesday nights, we gathered together at a mutual friend's house with lots of food, fellowship, and worship. I had developed a large group of friends and was enjoying single life in my thirties. As a leader in my group, which met on Friday nights, I felt as if it was my responsibility to lead the single people to Jesus. I told them that their main focus should be to develop their walk in the Lord and to make themselves available to do ministry in the church. I taught Bible study with that as a foundation. Well, some didn't want to hear that. They wanted to know about "Christian Dating." I never heard of "Christian Dating" until one of the men mentioned it.

He went to the pastor and he became the leader. All these carnal Christians wanted to know was how far they could go without sinning and getting pregnant. Their philosophy was, "How are you going to get to know somebody if you don't date?" And my main point was, "Seek first the Kingdom of God." Therefore, I left that ministry. About a week later, a woman called me on the phone crying because she let one of the men kiss her. She was upset because the man didn't want to marry her. Of course I gave her the "I Told You So" speech as gentle as I could. She received my advice and now she is happily married to the man God brought in her life. Not too long after the battle and church split at this non-denominational church, my mother and I went back to the Assemblies of God church.

Years later, after our pastor retired, a young pastor was hired and a lot more married couples joined the church with their children, which was a good thing; however, I started feeling Desperate and Envy again. This new pastor decided to have the members of the congregation fill out a survey called "Holy Spirit Gifts and You." In the survey, the members had to answer a list of questions concerning their likes, dislikes, and what they enjoyed and didn't enjoy doing. After the score was tallied, the survey told us what Gift that God had placed on our lives. My highest score was in the Gift of Celibacy. I could not believe my ears: "What? That can't be right because God told me I'm getting married!" After the pastor disclosed my score from that survey to the office staff, they teased me and gave me a home-made card with a picture of an empty island on it and some words typed on it. The only word I saw on the card was "CELIBACY." They laughed and thought it was a joke. That started an emotional stumble, a roll down a hill into depression for me.

My Calling:
When I Said No To God

One evening as I was reading my Bible, the words in Matthew 19: 11-13 spoke to me: "For there are some eunuchs, which were so born from their mother's womb: and there are some eunuchs, which were made eunuchs of men: and there be eunuchs, which have made themselves eunuchs for the kingdom of heaven's sake. He that is able to receive it, let him receive it." I responded, "I can't receive it!" After that, a few married women said, "Sometimes God doesn't call people to marry." Well, that statement angered me; therefore, I started arguing, "Who do they think they are telling me I'm not called to get married? Here they are happily married and they are going to tell me this! Besides, marriage is *not a calling!*" For years I argued against this calling on my life. Then one day I said to the pastor, "I'm called of God to be single." He said, "Better you than me." And there I stumbled again and rolled down the emotional hill again. Why this time because Envy brought in Rejection.

At this point now, thirty- five years old, I just graduated from a two-year college with my Associate of Arts Degree in Theatre. I thought, "Now I will be able to meet my husband." Not! I couldn't even find a job. So I went back to school for a duel Bachelor of

My Calling

Arts degree in Theatre and Art. In 1995, I graduated and still no meeting of the man of my dreams and getting married. I started tutoring English and teaching a two-credit course at Camden County College still feeling unsatisfied and unfulfilled. Because I was in God's permissive will by not accepting my calling, my soul was in so much agony from the confusion and fears that my body became ill. I developed a chronic allergy of coughing, sneezing, and itching all over and I was diagnosed with tumors in my uterus that just kept on growing no matter how much I prayed. In May 2001, 38 years after I heard the words "You are getting married", the Holy Spirit led me to buy a book called *Come Away My Beloved* that has a poem in it based on the book in the Bible called *Songs of Solomon*. The poem is filled with words of love and affection; hence, we consummated our marriage.

On the night of July 15, 2001, I recorded in my journal when "The Lord rubs and kisses my eyes and tells me to open them: 'Open your eyes and look at Me. Tell Me what you see. Come away My beloved.' He's taking me with Him." Then on July 16th, while reading Isaiah 54: 5, the words "Thy Maker is thine Husband" stood out to me as if Jesus, Himself, spoke to me. I gladly received those words in my heart until one day I realized that meant there definitely was not going to be a man to marry. Later on that year, the Lord came to me and sat next to me on my bed. Feeling unworthy to look at Him, I turned my back to Him and asked, "Why are you here?" He said, "Because I love you." So I thought, "Uh, oh! It's more to it than that. Something is about to happened." And it did!

While tutoring at Camden County College (CCC), I went on to study Writing with a concentration in Composition and Rhetoric on the Master degree level as I was encouraged to further my education. At this same time, my mother was diagnosed with colon cancer and she became very ill. She made it to my graduation in May 2002; however, in January 2003, she passed away. I was left on this earth with no ancestors and no generations. My sister and her children had disappeared out of my life for too many years. In January, 2003, for the first time in my life, I felt alone. I lost my mind. I was angry at God, angry at the government of this country, and I hated a few board members of the church who turned their backs on me. After several months passed, one summer evening during the mid-week service, one of the deacons said, "We cared about your mother. But you, we don't care about!" I was deeply wounded in my soul that I did not eat for fifty-seven days.

Finally, after I passed out several times, I called the pastor and asked him to take me to the hospital. God kept me! My body did not suffer at all, even with the massive tumor in my uterus. After I returned to my mother's house from the hospital, I had to settle the estate. Well, that was very challenging to me. My mother left me with two cars and a house still in her name. We both paid for everything together. Now what do I do without her? So again, there I was stumbling and rolling down on the steep hill into depression. Only this time Desperation and Rejection introduced me to Deception.

There was a man, brother in Christ, in my life at the time as a dear friend. His mother and my mother became friends through him. For the Thanksgiving Holiday, a year before my mother left this earth, my mother and I spent the holiday with him and his large, friendly, warm-loving family. We enjoyed the holiday and we enjoyed spending time with this family. The night my mother went Home, this brother in the Lord spent hours on the phone with me

My Calling

because I was grieved that my mother passed and my sister hung up the phone on me when I called to talk to her. That night and for several weeks, he called me every night. Well, one night when he called, I heard the words, "He is your husband." I told the brother what I had heard and he thought I was making it up. I said, "No, this is what I heard in the phone while you were talking!" After this brother had married another woman, moved west, and had a child, I heard the words, "He is your husband." Every time I heard these words I kept saying, "No he is not!" Devil you are a liar!" He is not the answer to my prayer; he is not my heart's desire!"

Right before the spring semester started at Camden County College, I went to the College to tell the Tutor Center coordinator what hours I would be available. Before I could utter another word, I said, "Oh, wow! I better wait. I just dreamt that I passed out." She said, "Are you okay?" I said, "I'm fine." I drove myself home, walked in the house, and sat on the couch. Instantly, I fell asleep. Not realizing I slept on the couch the whole night, I awoke and called the coordinator to cancel my schedule for the semester. She said, "Okay. Do you want to go to the hospital?" I said, "Yes."

While I was in the hospital, the surgeon gave me a total hysterectomy. I was castrated! I had lost all hope and dreams. The surgeon said that the tumor in my uterus was 44 pounds and my sugar was 2000. While in the hospital, the nurses gave me pain medication, and yet I did not suffer any pain. However, one evening while lying in the bed, I saw something strange. I saw a presence slowly leave my body. I asked the Lord, "Is there another part of me?" He instantly gave me knowledge that it was a demon spirit. Several weeks went by before I was able to leave the hospital and go home.

Just before my mother's house went to foreclosure, I moved out, resigned my membership from the Assemblies of God church and stayed several weeks with a couple from the church. While living with this couple, I finally broke down and cried uncontrollably. I suffered loss: my mother, her house, a part of my body, and my dream of getting married and having children. In January 2007, I moved into my apartment. On February 19TH, I was diagnosed with End Stage Renal Disease and placed on dialysis. Moving into my apartment was a new beginning for me. I figured now I would meet this man of my dreams, and that God would restore my body. Looking for a church home, I started visiting other churches. Everywhere I went, I heard this question in my mind, "Is he here?" "Is he here?" That question was tormenting. I started looking for a husband; however, there wasn't a single man around that remotely was what I was looking for and none were attracted to me.

Finally, summer of 2007, I joined a deliverance church that had a Single's Ministry. At the same time I was still fellowshipping with this brother in the Lord, my friend over the phone. For eleven years, this brother called me to tell me about the mistake he made in marrying this woman who turned out to be a liar. She told him that she was a Born-again Christian; then after they were married, she got tired of the Christian mask she wore, took it off, and showed her real face. Through those eleven years, I diligently prayed for him asking the Father in the name of Jesus to help him, to vindicate him from the troubles that were coming his way through all of the battles. This man was going through! So I said, "It's been twelve years now and I keep hearing the same message that this brother is my husband. Maybe God is telling me that this man is my husband. He's not who or what I'm praying for, but if this is God's will then I have to say okay." Even though I said this, I still questioned the message because God promised to give me the desire of my heart.

Well, that night as I lay on my bed praying in the spirit, the anointing of God was on me and I saw out of my peripheral view a large figure walking towards me. I closed my eyes and shouted, "Okay! He is not my husband!" and continued praying in my prayer language until I fell asleep. That was twelve years of deception and I thank God for deliverance! Here is where my argument started. I still struggled with God's Call on my life; however, what I noticed was the pastors of this Deliverance church were encouraging the young single people to pray to get married instead of to seek after God's will for their lives. One Friday evening, he asked, "Why do you want to get married?" Several people had different answers. At the same time he stood before the Single's congregation and bragged about how his life was so wonderful being married to his wife as the wife blushed and giggled. He then repeated the question, so I answered, "Because two are better than one." Suddenly, one of the married women turned to me and said, "Well, sometimes God calls some people not to marry."

For the first time that statement didn't bother me as much as it did in the past. However, the pastor disregarded her statement with a statement: "But, if you were stuck on the road and had a flat tire, you gonna need some help!" He thought what he said was funny; nobody else did. The congregation felt too intimidated by the pastor to make any more rebuttals. Every fourth Friday of the month was the same thing. It was as if Lust was in the sanctuary. All he focused on was dating and getting married. I became so tired of listening to him that I decided not to attend any more meetings.

Then I argued, "If it's God's will for some not to marry, why is that not taught in the church?" We all learn about the Call of God: apostle, prophet, evangelist, pastor, and teacher, and even helps ministries, but nobody teaches about the Call of God not to marry.

I often heard that the divorce rate in the church is just as high as the divorce rate of people not in the church. If we were taught that some of us would be called by God to be celibate and/or to be married to Him, maybe about half of the people would not have gotten married. For almost thirty years, I struggled with wanting to be married. I prayed my "Prayer for a Husband" from a little prayer book and added some of my own words with scripture verses. I even encouraged some other singles to make a list: spirit first, then soul with intellect, likes and dislikes, then body and family. However, I was praying to the wind. Why? Because it was never God's will for me to meet a man and marry. It's God's will, His Call, for me to be married to Him, for Him to be my Husband.

MY CALLING:
Finally, I Said Yes To God

After all the years of deception and vain dreams and prayers, I finally accepted the fact that I am married to Jesus. One Sunday, 2012, a visiting bishop preached at the Church of God in Christ where I am now a member. At the end of the service, he invited people to come forward for prayer. When it was my turn, he looked at me and said, "Now since you made your commitment, just say, 'Thank You.'" I have embraced God's Calling on my life to be married to my Maker. So now I call myself "A Nun in the Protestant Church." I'm still amazed and I have peace in my soul. So many

Born-again believers have prayed to God for healing, financial increase, or even to get married. We know that there are healing and prosperity scriptures in the Bible that we can use for prayer. But when it comes to getting married or making a decision to travel to another state or country, we must know what God's will is for our lives.

Knowing God's will is to be intimately acquainted with Him, so that He can place us on the path for our lives and direct us. Knowing God's will is to be intimately acquainted with Him, so that He can reveal what His Call is on our lives. Furthermore, knowing God's will is to be intimately acquainted with Him, so that we can understand His methods, the way He chooses to handle situations in our lives. Knowing God's will is to be intimately acquainted with Him, so that He can reveal His desires in our hearts. Knowing God's will is to be intimately acquainted with Him, so that we can understand and keep the Love commandment and live by it. This is living a successful life. Some people think that the "Faith Movement" preachers are false teachers because they tried living by faith and it didn't work for them. Some think that it works for these pastors because they have a special call on their lives. I learned that some preachers do take some of the teachings of Faith to the extreme because they think we create our own world. We can't create our own world, our own destiny.

Our God is the One Who has created our lives and destiny before the foundation of the world. We are predestined to be in His image and to fulfill His call on our lives. In the Amplified Bible, Ephesians 2: 10 says, "For we are God's [own] handiwork (His workmanship), recreated in Christ Jesus, [born anew] that we may do those good works which God predestined (planned beforehand) for us [taking paths which He prepared ahead of time], that we should walk in them [living the good life which He prearranged and made ready for us to live]. That job belongs to God! The extreme faith preachers don't preach about Psalms 127: 1 "Except the Lord builds the house, they labor in vain that build it: except the Lord keep the city, the watchman wakes but in vain." If we are praying to get married and it is not God's will, then we pray in vain. This is how some people get married, the marriage ends in divorce, and people, including children, get hurt. And again, I John 5: 14 tells us that we are certain that God hears and answers our prayers if we are praying His will. If we don't know what His will is in a situation, then we can pray, "Father, Your will be done in this situation." Just leave it at that and continue to seek first the Kingdom of God, and His righteousness, and all these things shall be added unto you (Matthew 6: 33). To conclude, Colossians 1: 9 reads "For this cause we also, since the day we heard it, do not cease to pray for you, and to desire that ye might be filled with the knowledge of His Will in all wisdom and spiritual understanding." And this I pray for all those who read my story.

REJECTION SURVIVOR

*R*ejection can be labeled as a disease of the soul. Dictionary.com tells me that to reject is to refuse to accept (someone or something); rebuff: *The other children rejected him.* Some children who are rejected grow up either feeling as a reject to society or they become the predators who reject others. Then there are those who overcome this disease. In my estimation, rejection is like a cancer of the soul. It tends to destroy the soul of the person's personality, gifts, dreams, talents, likes, and dislikes. People celebrate being cancer survivors. Today, I am celebrating being a "Rejection Survivor."

In April, 1955, my parents brought home a little baby girl, me. My mother said that I was a very happy baby and easy to take care of. She also said that I was my father's favorite, so here I am with my father's name, Andrea; however, I don't think my sister agreed with sharing my father's attention. This is when the rejection started in my life. In the first part of my book called "A Memoir: From Father to Father," I stated that in December 1960, Andrew Leroy Mings, my father, passed away. He died because of a brain tumor, leaving his wife, Lillian Josephine and two daughters, Rochelle Antoinette and Andrea Denise. My sister was seven years old at the time, and I was five years old. After the sorrowful event of the funeral and the repass, my mother continued with our family rituals, but it just wasn't the same without my father. She had to become father and mother to her children. Not long after my father passed, in either February or March of 1961, my mother stopped going to church, but she continued to send my sister and me to Sunday school and to church.

On Saturdays, my mother washed, straightened, and curled my and my sister's hair. We had to wear sponge rollers to bed at night. What torture! Then one Sunday morning, after we ate breakfast, put our Sunday best clothes on, we combed our hair in the bathroom standing in front of the mirror over the sink. I can remember this one morning when Jealousy told my sister to splash water on my hair. When she did, I said, "What are you doing?" as loud as I could. She said, "Shss, shss! I'm sorry!" Then she took a towel and quickly wiped the water out of my hair in fear of my mother's wrath. Even though we shared some play time together, the rejection in my life started at home when I was very young by my own sister. Then there was the extended family.

Every year on Christmas Day, the family gathered at my great-grandmother's house. My mother bought my sister and me baby dolls and allowed us to take our dolls with us to show our family. When we arrived at my great-grandmother's house, some family members were already there. As we entered the house, there were the greetings and the "Oh-h-h's" and the "Ah-h-h's" as they encouraged my sister and me to model our new clothes and our new dolls. Well, Jealousy entered one cousin's heart. This particular cousin used to babysit my sister and me. We bonded; I felt connected to her. She also bought her daughter a baby doll, but for some reason, she became malicious. She cornered me and said, "That's an ugly doll!" I felt the evil for a split second then I walked away.

I told my mother what my cousin said, and my mother reprimanded her in front of everybody. However, the attack of rejection lingered in my memory and the bond between us was broken. Another form of rejection I experience was in the early sixties, when my sister and I went to Hamilton Elementary School together. My sister was told to walk me to school and don't be late. One morning my mother left a small pile of change (nickels, dimes, quarters, and pennies) on the dining room table. While my mother was upstairs getting dressed for work, my sister placed a dime under her tongue. So I yelled, "Uoo, Mommy! Toni took a dime off the table!" Toni yelled, "No I did not! You're a liar!" When she said "liar", the dime flipped in her mouth and she had to spit it out and put it back on the table. While my mother yelled at us for being late for school from upstairs, my sister and I walked out of the house.

When we walked to the corner of my street, my sister stopped and pretended as if she was banging her head against a stone wall and said, "I'm going to keep doing this until you say I'm sorry." Well, of course, in my mind's eye, I saw her head bleeding and blood on the wall, so I urgently said, "Sorry!" Then she hit me and ran to school leaving me to walk by myself. I was only in the first grade and I was very nervous. For the first time I had to walk alone. Moreover, throughout my elementary school years, for some reason, I developed enemies. I was a quiet, shy little girl who was uncomfortable in elementary school. Well, of course, there were the bullies. In second grade, one girl, named Veronica, decided she wanted somebody she could let out her frustrations on, so she picked me. One day during Arts and Crafts, she hit me while the teacher was not looking, so I hit her back.

This girl punched me in the stomach so hard that I lost my breath for a second. The teacher turned around to look at me but said nothing. Another day during recess, when Veronica realized that a boy, named Richard, from our class was interested in me, after school, she took his belt and started running towards me swinging the buckle of the belt. Well, of course, I ran until I left the school grounds. I turned and noticed that she stopped chasing me at the gate. Thank God I could run fast! Several days later, another girl, named Constance, decided she wanted to fight me. She sent me a note in class to invite me to fight her after school. I sent her the note back to ask her why. She did not respond and we never met.

Then in the sixth grade, a girl named Diane, who I had made friends with since the third grade, decided she wanted to fight me after school. This girl didn't have a reason why she wanted to fight me. So I met her after school right outside the gate of the school grounds. When we started to fight, I accidently tore her dress. We didn't wear pants to school during those days. Well, she was upset and started fussing about her dress: "When my mother sees this, I'm going to be in trouble!" Then she came after me. I was a fast runner in those days. While she chased after me, I ran to her house to apologize to her mother for tearing the dress. When the girl saw me at her house, she ran towards me so I ran home.

Not only did I encounter bullying in elementary school, I had encountered more bullies in junior high school. In Sayer Jr. High, a few girls in my section of the seventh grade class the first week of school decided they didn't like me. Why? I don't know! So my teacher switched me to another section. A few girls in the new section heard about why I was switched, so they decided to taunt and bully me. In fact, this time there were two of us in my class who were bullied, so the girls decided to encourage the one girl, named Gwendolyn, to pick a fight with me. Consequently, one day after class, she said, "Meet me after school." I said, "Okay, where?" She picked a place, but I said, "No. Meet me at my house."

After school, the street in front of my house was packed with people–children and adults. All came out to see the fight. My mother tried to reason with the girl, but she decided she wanted to fight; therefore, my mother stepped out of the way and let me at her. Right in front of my house, there was a large tree. This girl was much bigger than I, so she grabbed my hair and swung me around. Somehow I managed to pull away from her. I think one of the older boys in the neighborhood tried to separate us. She started swinging her fist and tried to punch me in the mouth, but for some reason her hand opened in my mouth; then in my inner ear I heard the word, "Bite." So I bit down as hard as I could like a bull dog. That finger was no good by the end of the fight.

The bullies who encouraged the fight were supposed to jump in the fight and beat on me but they all ran. Well, that fight gave me a reputation and a nick-name. The neighborhood teenagers started calling me Crazy Ange. After that fight, more neighborhood teenagers took an interest in me; therefore, on the weekends, after I finished my chores, my mother allowed me to go outside and socialize with them. We sat on each other's front steps and shared in conversation together peacefully. We laughed and talked and teased each other for hours. My mother told me that some of the neighborhood girls enjoyed me to the point that they used to ask if I could come outside. This is when Jealousy again walked into my sister's life, which caused her to reject me. It had gotten so bad that she used to go to my mother with lies and say that I was doing something immoral. My sister fabricated stories so many times that I remember hearing my mother say, "She can't be that bad! I don't believe she's that bad!"

During my high school years on the weekends, after my sister went away to college, I used to either go to a party or I used to have a party at my house. This was around the time when my friends started coupling together and dating; however, none of the boys were interested in me. I was born with my mother's large lips and my father's almond shaped eyes because there is Chinese in my ancestry and his teeth (a gap between front teeth). On top of that, I sucked my thumb, so that caused my teeth to protrude. In 1973, when the Violent family moved into our neighborhood across the street from my house on the corner of Samson and Alden Streets, the boys in that family made fun of my eyes, my lips, and my teeth. That's when I discovered why the boys in the neighborhood did not want to date me. Now here is where the rejection started hurting on the inside and I developed an inferiority complex. From that time on, all I wanted in life was to have someone who would like me as I was. In high school, there were boys I liked, but none liked me. Finally, at the age of eighteen, after I graduated from high school, my mother decided to move to South Jersey.

When we moved to South Jersey, I felt like I would have a fresh start. I remember standing outside on the balcony of our apartment one night and shouting, "I should have been born out here!" I felt free for the first time. I met new people who all became my friends; however, they were all coupled. I hung out with them for a couple of years anyway, feeling like the third party-social reject. I had a boyfriend, but all he really wanted was sex. I dumped him and continued my cry for a boyfriend. When I turned twenty-one, I decided to join the United States Army. I joined the U.S. Army for several reasons: to grow-up, to learn about me, and to get away from home. When I first left home and arrived at the Recession Station at Fort Jackson, South Carolina, it was exciting, an adventure.

Wow! Meeting new people, I decided to break out of the inferiority complex shell I was in. I became wild. I got tired of the rejections, so I decided to have fun. I had boyfriends, not realizing all they wanted was sex, and in a sense, I did not care; however, my answer was "No." After a week of staying at the Recession Station, we went to our Basic Training duty stations where we were separated into our barracks. Then one day, during my boot camp training, I discovered I was being rejected. In fact, it was a group of women who were being rejected. The drill sergeants in my platoon decided they did not want these women and found ways to get rid of them. Because I was friends with two of them, I was also targeted.

One woman was tough. She seemed as if she was from a gang infested area of a city, and the other was a sweet woman who was into eating natural foods and refused to eat the food the Army cafeteria served. She used to somehow sneak off the grounds and go to the grocery store to buy food. She introduced me to eating almonds and raisins together as a snack. Anyway, all of a sudden, they both disappeared, but I graduated from boot camp training by threating to expose my drill sergeants to the lieutenants. On the first day of boot camp training, the GI's were told not to fraternize with the drill sergeants. Well, my drill sergeants – men and women

–partied with a group of women: sex and homo-sex. I was invited to the parties, but I said, "No!" Since they knew that I was aware of the parties, they made sure I graduated. My drill sergeants rushed me through my entire Basic Training Drill final test and marked it as accomplished.

Then I had to get dressed in my best dressed military outfit and march in a parade. Marching in the parade was exciting. When we passed the section of the bleachers where the high rank officers sat, I heard my drill sergeant say, "Eyes right!" At that time we all in a uniform style had to look in that direction and salute while marching. I was so excited, I had chills. But wait. There's more. After the parade, I had to pack my clothes and personal items because I was being shipped to Fort Sam Houston in San Antonio, Texas. My Military Occupation Specialty (MOS) was Medical Laboratory Technician. I was being trained to test blood and to perform blood transfusions.

After several weeks of classes, I worked in a laboratory where the students had to draw each other's blood to test and discover the blood type (A, B, AB, or O), and to discover whether if the type was positive or negative. Then we were given test tubes with red blood cells in them. We had to match the blood with the blood we had drawn from each other. We did this several times for practice. At the end of class, my MOS sergeant said, "Well Private Mings, you just killed ten people." I was in shock! I swallowed hard, my jaw dropped, and I just stared at him. I didn't know what else to do. And there was nothing I could do. After class it was the routine chow time in the cafeteria, social time, then bed time.

On the day of the test, we had to perform blood test as practiced. Well strangely, right in the middle of the test, we were told to go to dinner. In the cafeteria, several of the women told me that the MOS sergeant was going to switch my test tubes so that I would fail the test. After dinner, when I went back to the lab to finish my test, I didn't know which tubes they switched, so I just completed my test. At the end of class, my MOS sergeant announced the names of all those who passed the test and my name was on the list. The MOS sergeant looked at me with astonishment. His face turned red. He couldn't figure how I did it. I know now. God did it for me. He is so good!

 The only reason they were able to get rid of me was that one day I discovered I had crabs crawling in my pubic hairs. I panicked and ran to the bathroom to pick them off of me. Not realizing how much time it took me to get rid of them, I was late for breakfast. I ran to the cafeteria only to discover that the platoon leader reported me as absent without leave (AWOL). So to punish me, they took me out of my MOS as a Medical Laboratory Technician at Ft. Sam Houston, and they sent me to Fort Leonard Wood, Missouri. The GI's there called it "Fort Lost in the Woods, Misery". There, my MOS was Mechanics. What?! I could not believe it. I had to sleep in the women's barracks and train with the men.

 Every morning I had to get up get dressed and run to my duty station. The reason I ran so fast was that there were skunks on the path. I could smell the strong odor. Since I had to march with the men, my MOS sergeant put me at the end of the line so that the men's eyes were not drawn to me while marching. In an in direct way, he let me know he didn't like me. By this time, I figured there must be something negative written on my documents that was causing these sergeants to dislike me. After a while, between running from skunks, marching with men, and fixing trucks, my body was tired and I started hemorrhaging. I couldn't stand straight or march, so they finally found a reason to discharge me (kick me out) from the Army. I was very angry. I carried that anger for years.

I was in the Army from April 1976 to June 1977, just fourteen months. It seemed much longer. Also, I was greatly disappointed because I had decided in my heart that I was going to meet Mr. Right while in the Army, which didn't happen. Unfulfilled, I arrived home to South Jersey in June 1977, but I had an urge not to stay home. One of my girlfriends, Denise, also was ready to leave home, so with her credit cards and my car, we headed for Los Angeles, California. She picked Los Angeles because she wanted to go to Hollywood and become a movie star. We were on the road for four days. It's funny. My mother said, "Don't stop anywhere down south." Well, it was in Alabama when I drove over something and flattened the right rear tire.

We were on Interstate 65, a four lane highway, going southwest in the middle of the night. I had no idea how to fix a flat tire. I knew that the bumper jack was to fit on the bumper, but for some reason I kept putting the bumper jack on the side of the car over the tire; therefore, it was not working. About fifteen to twenty minutes of trying to figure out how to use the jack, a school bus stopped on the road across from us going in the opposite direction. I saw the lights on the bus being turned off and then turned on several times. Then the driver stepped off the bus and started walking over to us. He told us that all of a sudden his bus just stopped. Then he noticed that we were stranded with the car so he came over to fix it. He changed the tire and bid us a good night. When he walked back across the highway and got back on the bus, I heard when the bus started up and he drove away. There was nothing wrong with the bus.

I was also relieved because Denise was fearful of the man and whispered to me, "Don't give the man the jack. I don't trust him." I gave the man the jack and after he fixed the tire, he told us he was coming from a revival at a church. My Father God was all the while watching over us. After several hours of driving on Interstate 10 following a truck driver doing about 90 miles an hour, we arrived in San Antonio, TX. While I was in the Army, I was stationed in San Antonio, so I knew some people to stay with. Here's is where my car was destroyed. The woman I stayed with, her boyfriend destroyed my car thinking she was cheating on him; therefore, Denise and I went on to Los Angeles by Greyhound bus. She quickly found a boyfriend. How do they do this?

Anyway, for the first couple of days, we stayed at a cheap motel until we found an apartment. It took me a while, but I finally found a job and a boy-friend, or he found me; either way, I was not satisfied. At this point in my life, I started looking for somebody to marry, and this man did not meet my criteria. This was during the time when I was invited to go to a Bible Study by a woman on my job. It was the summer of 1978 on a Wednesday night when I rededicated my life to Jesus and started going to a non-denominational Pentecostal church. That is seventeen years later after I had accepted Jesus as my Savior on Resurrection Sunday 1961. When I started going to church, I sensed within me that God was telling me to dump the boyfriend, so I dumped the boyfriend. While going to church, I became a member of the Singles Ministry and I made new friends, male and female. I saw a few men who looked promising, but they didn't see me as someone to spend the rest of their lives with. That old rejection came back when many of those singles became couples.

Now I'm being rejected by men in the church; however, I still fellowshipped with this ministry. The summer of 1979, one of the members of the Singles Ministry had a pool party at his house. Everyone enjoyed each other laughing, talking, and eating. Being an introvert, I didn't share much in conversation; therefore, I went into the pool. The men at the party decided to play a game on me by holding me under water. Every chance I got to raise my head and breathe, one of the other men pushed my head under the water. Then they all got out of the pool laughing while I was totally embarrassed. Because I rode with one of the members to the party, I couldn't just get up and leave. And to top it off, they all, the men and the women, ignored me the rest of the day. Here I was just starting to go to church and was rejected.

I'm quite sure if I didn't have the Holy Spirit of God, I would have stopped going to church. It's only by the grace of God that I still kept going to church. I continued fellowshipping with the Single's Ministry still hoping that a brother in Christ would be interested in me. After two years and some months, my mother said it was time for me to come home; therefore, in December 1980, I booked a flight and travelled home. I felt empty and unsatisfied. I had such hope that I was going to find my Mr. Right. As the plane ascended, I cried as if I had lost a loved one. The people on the plane tried to console me, but I just finally fell into a deep sleep.

It was warm and sunny in December the day I left Los Angeles, but when I arrived at the Philadelphia International Airport, it was cloudy and freezing cold. I was joyful in my heart to see my mother and my grandmother who came to meet me at the airport. After being home for a couple of weeks, during a conversation between my mother and I, I learned that my sister told my mother that I was being promiscuous while living in Los Angeles. Consequently, my mother believed it, so she told me to come home. I was amazed that my mother would believe such a thing and that my sister would even say such a thing about me to my mother when I was the one who introduced them both to the Lord and they both accepted Jesus as their Savior a year before I came home. Not only that, since I had been home, my mother and I had a disagreement because she thought I wasn't looking hard enough for a job. She said, "Toni told me you just want my money!" Completely losing all restraint, I yelled, "What?! You don't have any money!" Shocked at my response, my mother stared at me and said nothing. It took some time, but I had to win my grandmother and my mother over from the lies of my sister.

As I was led by the Holy Spirit of God, I decided to get braces for my teeth and become a student at Temple University. I started feeling better about myself, even though I still was looking for Mr. Right. As time went on, more disagreements arose between my mother and I while I was a student in college because she wanted me to find a job. I told her that everywhere I went, somebody was just hired. She didn't believe me, so she decided to go with me to several business and retail establishments only to get the same response I was getting: "Sorry, we just hired someone yesterday." Hence, I said, "I guess God wants me to go to college." When I decided to transfer to Camden County College, the Lord opened the door for me to get a job driving school buses. I drove a big yellow school bus every morning to pick up children and take them to school. Then while they were in school, I took classes at

Camden County College. By the time I finished my classes, it was time for me to go pick them up from school.

After I drove my students home from school, I then drove back to the bus depot, parked the bus, and then went back to the college to do my homework. Then from there on Wednesday nights, I went to church. Through the years, what I had discovered was that I was in God's will for my life, but the enemy was using my family against me. Once in a while, when my sister called home, I would share the love of God with her, but she would take it the wrong way, yell at me on the phone, and then hang up on me. And my mother, she gossiped about me in church with her friends to the point that one evening after school, when I went to church for Wednesday night Bible study, one of her friends said, "How are you doing?" I said, "I'm a little tired right now." He said, "Why? You don't work!" Amazed at his response, I said to him, "Yes I do! I work and I go to school." He said, "Oh!" and sheepishly walked away. I told my mother what happened; therefore, out of her guilt, she decided to announce all over the church that I work and I give her my whole paycheck, which I did.

For many years, I was angry and unforgiving towards my mother and my sister. Then one day, after my mother battled with diarrhea for a couple of months, she visited her doctor who ran some test only to discover that she had colon cancer. By this time, I had graduated and transferred to the university. I tried helping her at home, but I could not take off from work and school; therefore, a woman from the church decided to help by taking her to her doctor's appointments and to chemo therapy. Even though we lived in the same house, my mother stopped holding conversations with me. All she did at home was sit and watch TV.

After I graduated from college with my master's degree from the university, I went with her to her doctor's appointment. He asked me if I wanted to see her x-rays, and I reluctantly said, "Yes." He showed me that the cancer had spread all through her body and in her brain. So I thought, "This is why all she did was stare at the TV and didn't hold any conversations."

Also, my mother started doing things that didn't make any sense; for example, one time I found a carving knife in the oven, and another time she asked one of her friends to buy her some food from the supermarket, when we had already gone shopping. One evening, after I noticed that she had been sitting in one spot all day staring at the TV, I called the pastor and he told me to take her to the hospital. I said, "Mommy, you're going to the hospital." I called the care taker over to help me get her dressed. Her feet were so swollen that we couldn't put her shoes on. The whole time we were dressing her she cried and said, "I don't want to go to the hospital." The care taker came with me as I drove my mother to the hospital. The hospital took her in, ran some test, and decided there was nothing more to do for her. The hospice nurse came to my mother's room to talk to me and to explain that I could put her in the nursing home or take her home. The Lord told me not to take her home. When I told my mother this, she said, "Well, that's it for me."

While my mother was at the nursing home, I prayed for two days when suddenly, the Holy Spirit said, "Go and tell your mother to ask the Father for forgiveness." I urgently went to the nursing home and said, "The Lord said you need to ask the Father to forgive you." As she cried, she prayed for forgiveness. She did not look at me the whole time. Not too long after that I left. The next day I visited her with the pastor. She did not look at me the whole time or say a word. At twelve midnight, I received a phone call that said, "Your mother just passed away." I called my sister as soon as I got the message and my sister, or her husband at the time, picked up the phone and then hung it up. I froze for a second; then I sat on a chair and cried like a baby for hours. At that moment, the Holy Spirit asked me, "Do you need some help? I said, "Yes." So He graciously moved my body to walk to the bathroom, to take a shower and to go to bed.

With the help of the church, the Memorial service was accomplished. The sanctuary was half filled with people who genuinely loved my mother, and my sister did show up for the service. I was very angry because again I felt abandoned by my mother and my sister. I was abandoned when I was a teen and now I was being abandoned again. My sister and my cousin left me to take care of all this by myself. No family was around to help. I was angry at the church because right after the Memorial Service, one of the deacons said, "Your mom we care about, but we don't care about you." Another woman said, "Your mother's gone now. What are you going to do?" I angrily responded, "I took care of my mother!" She said, "Okay. I was just kidding!"

Not only that, another woman from the church told me that my mother held a conversation with her the same night she passed away. Conclusion, my mother rejected me on her death bed. I was angry at my mother and my sister, I was angry at the government because of all I had to go through with the estate, and I was angry at God for allowing all of this to happen me and because He did not create a man who would want to love me and marry me. I was alone and so angry that I drove my mother's car from

South Jersey to North Jersey, until the car ran out of gas. Then for hours that night, I walked and walked and walked until the police picked me up and sent me to a mental hospital. I was so beaten down by rejection that I even accused God for rejecting me. At that time, I said, "What's the point in me living?" After several weeks of being in the mental hospital, I called one of the deacon's wives and told her where I was located. She came to visit me, and with strong persuasion, she talked the pastor into helping me to get out from the hospital and to get me back into my mother's house. I lived in my mother's house until it went into foreclosure.

Then a compassionate couple from the church allowed me to stay with them for a few weeks, and the husband helped me to get an apartment. Through teachings about love and forgiveness from the Holy Spirit, I learned that no matter how people treat me, I'm only hurting myself if I choose not to forgive. Therefore, I forgive my family and all those who had wronged me. Because of fear and because I was in sin by being so angry and by harboring unforgiveness, I not only lost my mind from all of the rejection, I lost a part of my body. I prayed for healing, but my prayer was not answered. In 2006, my blood sugar was 2000, and I had to have a radical hysterectomy because of a tumor that grew to 44 pounds in my uterus. In 2007, a few days after I moved into my apartment, I was diagnosed with End Stage Renal disease. The doctor asked the head nurse, "Will her kidneys ever come back?" Before I could open my mouth, she blocked me from speaking and shook her head to the doctor. I am now on hemodialysis 3 days a week for 6 years, and every day I praised and thank God for my day of deliverance, for now I know my prayer has been answered.

Also, I thank God and give Him all the glory because the power walk, pacing back and forth in my apartment, caused me to lose weight. I was wearing size 14 and now I am a size 6. Hallelujah! Moreover, I am so grateful to the Holy Spirit for teaching me to be at peace with God and satisfied with His will for my life. I have accepted my calling to be celibate and to be His wife. Because of Him, my soul is healed and I am free.

THE JOURNEY TO DISCOVER MY ASSIGNMENT

*A*s I mentioned early, after my father passed in December 1960, my family Sunday ritual of going to church ended. From the early to the mid 1960's, my weekend morning ritual was to get up, eat a bowl of cold cereal and watch cartoons, then go outside and play for a couple of hours after I did my chores. On some weekends we went to Atlantic City, but our Sunday ritual was to visit our grandparents for the day and watch television dramas including *Gun Smoke* and *The Rifleman,* filmed in the late 1950's, *and the Big Valley starring Barbara Stanwyck*, which was filmed in the mid 1960's. After we came home from my grandparents' house, we watched movies that were either musicals or western movies on television such as *Seven Wives for Seven Brothers* that was filmed in 1954 or one of our favorite John Wayne movies such as *Rio Bravo* filmed in 1959. I didn't watch a movie or TV drama just for the sake of entertainment. While lying in my bed at night before I went to sleep, I would visualize myself in the costumes and imagine myself on the set socializing with the other actors according to the way I would have written the scene and the dialogue. The movies and dramas sparked in me a creative urge to write. Also when I was sixteen, I was very impressed with my girlfriend who wrote poems. Her talent was writing, knowing how to express her deepest thoughts in words and put them on paper.

Several times I tried writing poetry, but the poems I wrote were very bawdy. I used to take a letter from the alphabet and write a story using that one letter about a fictional character in several stanzas. It all rhymed! However, deep down inside, I still was not satisfied. There was a part of me that wanted to say something. In my early twenties, when I went back to church, I told God I wanted to express my deepest thoughts on paper, and I prayed He would help me do this. I wanted to write! For about ten to fifteen years, I kept a journal of all my prayers, dreams, and deepest thoughts. I also kept another journal where I saved all of my notes from Sunday sermons that actually spoke to my heart so I could take time to mediate on them. God answered my prayers! He helped me get these journals started and He helped me place words on paper that expressed my inner self. My soul was satisfied. This experience shaped my future.

After graduating from high school in 1974 from Lincoln College Preparatory School in Philadelphia, Pennsylvania, God told me to go to college. In 1981, while attending Temple University in Philadelphia, I decided to study Theatre, but I discovered that I had to first pass a basic skill writing class. On the first day of the basic skill class, my instructor introduced herself to the class, told us about the Writing Lab, gave us a few brief instructions, and then dismissed us. Two of the instructions she mentioned were that the students had to meet in the lab during the scheduled class time and not to leave the lab until we have finished writing our essays. She also said that the students had the opportunity to test out of the class by midterm if the committee accepted our essays. From that first day of class until the middle of the semester, my instructor was not available to see the students, and she did not give us any instruction as far as how to write or what was expected. For the second class meeting, I went to the writing lab as instructed, which was located in a lecture hall. I entered the room, sat at a desk and noticed in front of the classroom there was a long list of topics on the chalkboard. The students were told to choose a topic from the list and write. Since this experience happened many years ago, I don't remember the topics; however, what I can remember is that the long list of topics was all about personal experiences.

    I struggled with being an introvert; therefore, I felt intimidated by the topics, and I struggled with the fear of exposure. I also felt as if I was being tested without being given any instruction. Consequently, I developed a writer's block. This was my second writing experience. For the next several class sessions, I sat in the writing lab, stared at the long list on the chalkboard, froze, and then left. I just did not know how and where to begin writing and what to write. While I was sitting in the writing lab for about the fifth time, I figured I better write something. I chose a topic using the "Eeny meeny miny moe" technique. When I started writing, I sat for the whole lab period writing whatever came to my mind. At the end of each period, I handed my paper to one of the monitors and exited the lab.

    During the middle of the semester, I met with my instructor who invited me into her office and offered me a chair to sit on. After a few polite greeting, she spread my essays on her desk and told me half of them were too specific and the other half were too general. I really wanted to tell her I thought that the topics were too personal, but I did not have the courage to say so. This instructor did not give me any advice as far as how to balance my ideas or how to write from general to specific. After our conference time, we politely exchanged a few closing remarks and parting gestures and I exited her office. I felt as if the instructor did not do her job and that made me angry. I wanted to complain to her superiors, but because of feeling empty and confused, I just walked away. At the end of the semester, I met with the instructor who told me the same thing because I made the same mistakes. In the final conference with her, she tried to put my papers in an order to try to figure out my life. She asked me personal questions such as, "How does this experience relate to this experience?" and "How did you do this if you couldn't do that?"

    I chose not to respond to her questions. I wanted to say, "None of your business!" Why? Because about half of what I wrote was fiction, and I really did not have an answer for her. We exchanged a few concluding remarks and gestures for parting, and I exited her office. The thing that I feared the most came upon me. I failed the class, but I did not allow this experience to discourage me from writing. For the following semester, I enrolled in another Basic Skill Writing class with a different instructor. With ardent determination, I decided to pass this class by the semester's midterm since I was forced to repeat it. At the beginning of the semester, the new professor gave the same instructions that I received from the previous instructor as far as the location of the Writing Lab and what to do in the lab. This instructor also gave his students some instructions

The Journey to Discover My Assignment

about what was expected from us in an essay and gave us a writing assignment for homework.

Now, I had an idea of what they were looking for. I'm not able to recall the topic of the essay, but I labored through prayer, and I used the dictionary and a thesaurus to make my essay look perfect. When I asked the Holy Spirit to help me understand my assignment and to help me write my essay, something blossomed inside of me. My assignment became clear, and I could actually visualize what I wanted to write. The next class session, when I handed the professor my essay, I felt confident he was going to be impressed with what I wrote and give me a good grade. I was right! He was very impressed to the point that he said, "Boy, your professor sure taught you a lot last semester!" Because he attributed the success of my essay to my former professor, anger filled my mouth. Restraining the full impact of an explosion, I said, "She didn't teach me anything!" He walked away and did not speak to me the rest of the class period.

For the next several class sessions, the students were instructed to go to the Writing Lab until midterm; then we were to return to the class for a class session, and not to an office as did my former instructor. For my last writing assignment in the lab, before midterm, I chose a topic that instructed me to write about something typical that happens to something or to me in my daily experience. I wanted this paper to be excellent. After I chose the topic, I asked to be excused to use the ladies' room. I went to the ladies' room and then to the Language Lab, which just happened to be empty. I went into the lab and prayed, "Father God, I ask that you help me write this essay in Jesus' name, amen." Before I left the lab, God gave me a vision of what to write. I went back to the Writing Lab and wrote about how my mother drove to work every morning and compared her to the Red Baron in the Peanuts cartoon. Again, I handed one of the monitors my essay with confidence.

During the final midterm class session, my professor gave my classmates their papers and told me the Committee was very impressed with my essay and was passing it around to the other English professors. Before that midterm week was over, I asked for my essay and the professor gave me another excuse. I was angry and disappointed at the same time because he refused to return my essay to me. To this day, as I am writing, I feel sad because I enjoyed writing that essay and it was well received by the professors. The main point is God answered my payer. Between classroom instruction and answered prayer, I passed the class and was able to enroll in College English Composition classes. Nevertheless, living in New Jersey and commuting back and forth to Temple University was too much for me, so I decided to go to Camden County College (CCC) in Blackwood, New Jersey. In the College Composition classes, I wrote with one goal in mind, the excellent paper, and I made good grades. However, I studied Theatre and graduated with an Associate degree from CCC in 1990. While studying, I wrote a ballet called *The Awakening: Joy Epidemic*.

From there, I transferred to Glassboro State College, which is now Rowan University, to complete my studies in Theatre thinking that this was God's call and assignment on my life; however, this was just a part of it. Studying Theatre was hard work. Theatre students didn't just take classes; we also had to participate in the shows. Some of the various jobs were: assisting the costume designer with selecting clothes and accessories for the actors; sewing, washing, and ironing clothes; assisting the technical director with using machines, tools, and paint brushes to build sets; and reading the script to select the properties, such as dishes, lamps, food, and a deck of cards that the actors would use while in character. Some of the other jobs were acting in the plays, assisting with the set, costume, and property changes, and stage managing. I volunteered to be the stage manager for the spring and fall theatre productions, and I volunteered to be an actor in the summer theatre productions. My goal for choosing these positions was to learn about directing and how to run a show. Also, one spring semester, I enrolled in a playwriting seminar class and learned that playwrights observe people, places, and events to create story lines and dialogues about what they observe. They also research topics or take stories from newspaper articles to create dialogues, or they develop dialogues from pictures or photographs. All of this answered my desire to write for the stage and film, and was leading me to my God-given assignment.

After graduating from Rowan University in 1995 with a double major degree in Theatre and in Art, I began directing one-act plays at the Christian Center in Blackwood, New Jersey. Twice a year, I wrote, casted, and directed illustrated sermons for the stage and video. Also, I was hired as a professional tutor at Camden County College (CCC) in Blackwood, New Jersey for basic skills and college writing. While tutoring, the coordinator and a colleague talked me into going back to college for my Master degree so that I would be able to teach writing at the college. I agreed, but I wasn't sure what writing style I wanted to use as an occupation, so I enrolled in a Journalism class and a Creative Writing class at

CCC. While studying Journalism, I joined the college's newspaper team, *Campus Press*, and wrote several articles for the paper. I was the Managing/ Copy-Editor one semester and the Editor-In-Chief the following semester. Several poems I wrote in the Creative Writing class were published in the College's literary magazine, *Bridges*. Upon completing these classes, it dawned on me that I had just completed the Communications curriculum, and for that reason, I graduated again from Camden County College in 1999.

During the summer of 1999, I spoke with the undergraduate communications advisor at Rowan University and she gave me information about the new Master's program for Writing Arts at Rowan. When I first enrolled, I thought about studying the Creative Writing and Journalism track, but since I was already a tutor for Basic Writing Skills and English Composition, I decided to study the Composition/Rhetoric track. As a student, I had several assignments where I had to write fiction and non-fiction stories, and without me realizing it, I had developed an unfinished manuscript. For thirteen years now, I have been teaching English Composition I and II at CCC.; however, it's only a part-time-temporary job. I prayed and tried several times to find a full-time job, and still for the past six years, no doors opened. Then the Lord said, "Take what you have in your hand." I remember reading in the Bible when God gave Moses a rod and through that rod, God worked signs over the Egyptians and as a result, the ten plagues and the parting of the Red Sea. However, I responded, "What do I have in my hand?" Then one day in August, 2012, as I passed by my incomplete manuscript, I realized Jesus was telling me to write my story and that Writing is my assignment and full-time job from Him. I like to say, "God hired me!"

As I wrote in the *Memoir: From Father to Father*, at a very early age, God became my Father. He protected me from all that the devil tried to destroy me with. The Bible says that we wrestle not against flesh and blood, but against demon spirits, according to Ephesians chapter six. Of course, it wasn't until I started going to church and was baptized in the Holy Spirit that I became aware of who the real enemy was, so I had to forgive my family and all the people who were used by those evil spirits to ruin my life. Later in my years, my God delivered me from all my fears, nightmares, and the evil spirits, so now I sleep soundly and peacefully. It is amazing to me that as a young teen, I had a deep desire to write, not knowing that Writing is actually my gift and assignment from God. Additionally, I am very grateful to my Husband, Lord Jesus, Who chose me to be His wife before the foundation of the world, and to the Holy Spirit of God, for loving me, for the work He has been doing in me, and for being so kind and patient with me when I resisted His promptings. He has definitely domesticated me and He is still at work in me designing His living sculpture.

In Loving Memory of My Parents

On December 3, 1960, Andrew Leroy Mings, veteran of the United States Army and a security guard at Holmesburg State Prison in Pennsylvania, died of a brain tumor, leaving his wife, Lillian Josephine and two daughters, Rochelle Antoinette and Andrea Denise. Before he passed on, he began teaching his oldest daughter, Rochelle at age 7, to read the Bible.

On January 2, 2003, at midnight, I received a phone call from the nursing home that Lillian Josephine Mings passed away. Born June 14, 1927, Litty Simpson was raised in South Philadelphia. In 1948, she married Andrew Leroy Mings. After her husband died, she went on to continue her life and became the first black woman to graduate from John Robert Powers Modeling School. Through the school, she became the spokes model for Coca-Cola Company radio commercials. She was offered more opportunities in the modeling business but refused them to stay home and raise her children. Instead, she started her own modeling school in her home. She and her mother, along with Lady Bug Fashion Boutique in Center City Philadelphia, gave fashion shows at various places in center city and in north Philadelphia. Moreover, she graduated from O.I.T Business School for Office Training and was hired at Temple University, where she was employed for twenty-seven years and was an active union representative. In 1979, I had the privilege to lead my mother to the Lord.

In 1981, my mother was baptized in the Holy Spirit at Deliverance Evangelistic Church. In 1982, she became a member of Bethel Tabernacle Assemblies of God, now known as Bethel Christian Center, under the leadership of Pastor Charles Scrimale in Mt. Ephraim, NJ., which is now located in Blackwood, NJ under the leadership of Pastor Kurt Kinney. She became involved in several ministries at the church including the choir. In 1995, Lillian Mings retired from Temple University and was led by the Holy Spirit to work in the church office at Bethel CC. and to be a ministry leader of Mending Wings, a ministry for hurting women. In 1998 Lillian Mings was diagnosed with a tumor in her colon and colon cancer. As time passed, the cancer spread throughout her body. No matter how much pain she was in, she smiled and greeted people in church. Through times of test and trials, my mother and I shared in fellowship, in the Word of God, in battles, and in victories. I was chosen by God to be the one to be with my mother when she was escorted to Heaven. December 29th, the horse and chariot came for her while she was in the hospital. After she left this earth, the Holy Spirit gave me a split second vision of my mother with a big smile on her face as a gentle looking hand was extended to her to usher her into the Presence of the Lord.

The Other Side of Death

The beauty of autumn is the end of a season.
The end of life is but for a reason.
These earthly bodies we will shed
to leave for decay in the grave yard bed.
Awaken from death to the promised eternal life
To streets paved with gold and the glassy sea.
We'll all give an account for the life and every breath
What a glorious day that will be!

www.ingramcontent.com/pod-product-compliance
Ingram Content Group UK Ltd.
Pitfield, Milton Keynes, MK11 3LW, UK
UKHW041954230426
12048UKWH00008B/333